Chamomile

Herb of the Year™ 2025

International Herb Association

Compiled and edited by Kathleen Connole

IHA Herb of the Year™

Each year the International Herb Association chooses an **Herb of the Year™** to highlight. The Horticulture Committee evaluates possible choices based on their being outstanding in at least two of the three major categories: culinary, medicinal, and ornamental. Herbal organizations around the world work together with us to educate the public throughout the year.

Herb of the Year™ books are published annually by the

International Herb Association
P.O. Box 5667 Jacksonville, Florida 32247-5667
www.iherb.org

This book is intended as an informational guide. The remedies, approaches, and techniques described herein are meant to supplement, and not to be a substitute for professional medical care or treatment; please consult your health care provider.

The International Herb Association is a professional trade organization providing education, service, and development for members engaged in all aspects of the herbal industry.

ISBN: 979-8-9878959-4-8

Uniting Herb Professionals for Growth
Through Promotion and Education

The International Herb Association has some of the most dedicated volunteers who keep the organization afloat, giving their time and talents to ensure that IHA continues to share herbal knowledge and connect those in the profession of herbs. We are deeply indebted to the IHA Board of Directors, the IHA Foundation members, and our webmaster. Thanks for all that you do and for caring enough to move us forward!

Acknowledgments

Chamomile Herb of the Year™ 2025 is an interesting follow up to *Yarrow Herb of the Year™ 2024* as it turns out they have much in common. Who knew that chamomile was a bitter herb? Most of us know of it as a gentle, sweet apple-scented tea, to be taken for more restful sleep or an upset tummy. As we learned from *Yarrow*, it is the bitterness that makes these plants powerful medicine.

Since there is more than one chamomile, Susan Belsinger explains the differences between the two most well-known, commonly called German and Roman, and relates her experiences growing them both side by side in her garden. She introduces us to some less familiar plants known as chamomile as well. Rosemary Davis gives us an overview of the chamomiles, describing folklore and historical uses through the ages. Karen England has fond memories of one of the chamomiles that some consider just a weed. Another similarity of chamomile to yarrow is that both are good used in companion planting; Diann Nance suggests that we keep this in mind as we plant our gardens. Jane Hawley Stevens shares her many years of experience growing, harvesting, and using chamomile on her central Wisconsin farm. Skye Suter writes of camomile (the English spelling) and its unique history in Tudor gardens, where it was grown as a lawn. Chuck Voigt spins a tale of chamomile that will leave those of us who lived through the 70s smiling. Growing chamomile in the Ozarks is a welcome sign of spring to Tina Marie Wilcox.

Chamomile as a culinary herb goes beyond the well-known tisane or tea in the creative kitchens of Susan Belsinger, Gert Coleman, Pat Crocker, and Rosemary Davis. Karen England gives us her always interesting take on using this Herb of the Year in spirited beverages.

Chamomile as a medicinal herb has many possibilities beyond tea and there are recipes for a variety of healthy formulations from Susan Belsinger and Gert Coleman, and lovely products for our health and beauty from Janice Cox. Daniel Gagnon dives deeply into the science of the medicinal properties and constituents of German chamomile, and offers advice on how to use this herb as medicine. Carol Little shares her experiences with chamomile in the home apothecary. The essential oils of the two most well-known chamomiles

have healing powers; Dorene Petersen provides an analysis of their properties and recipes for using them at home. Marge Powell gives us instructions on how to make a wonderful healing balm that she has used with good results for many years.

We have again been provided with many beautiful chamomile photographs by Susan Belsinger, Gert Coleman, Janice Cox, Pat Crocker, Karen England, Dorene Petersen, and Marge Powell; and illustrations by Pat Kenny, Alicia Mann, and Gail Wood Miller, without which the book would be much less interesting and pleasing to our eyes.

In this, my fourth year of editing the *Herb of the Year™* books, I am continuously reminded of how much there is yet to learn. My appreciation for all the time, expertise, and diversity of viewpoints given by each of our contributors has grown exponentially. The book would not be possible without all of their combined efforts.

This never-ending learning process of being editor would have been much less rewarding without the benefit of the assistance of second readers Susan Belsinger, Gert Coleman, and Karen Kalergis.

All these efforts would be for nought if we did not have Heather Cohen, talented graphic artist and layout expert. We can be confident that she will help us to produce another *Herb of the Year™* book that we can be proud of, that will stand the test of time.

It is sometimes a challenge for my family members to understand the obsessive behavior that occurs during the production of these books. I am very grateful for their tolerance, encouragement and support, without which it would not be possible.

~ Kathleen Connole

German chamomile blooms. Bartram's Garden, Philadelphia, Pennsylvania. *Pat Crocker*

Chamomile Botanical Nomenclature

Editor's Note: The chamomile that is commonly called German chamomile was given its Latin name by Linnaeus in 1753 in his work *Species Plantarum*. The accepted genus name given by Linnaeus is *Matricaria*; however, there are two species names that also date from 1753: *M. chamomilla*, or *M. recutita*. The botanical name *Matricaria chamomilla* is the current, first choice for correct botanical nomenclature. However, the synonyms *Matricaria recutita* and *Chamomilla recutita* are also used interchangeably. The former synonym *M. recutita* is seen more often in most sources and is widely used.

Table of Contents

Chamomile in the Kitchen

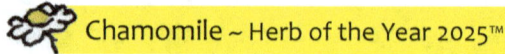

Health & Beauty

Soothing, sleep tisane
Tiny yellow and white blooms
Relax and sweet dreams

Susan Belsinger

katkenny

Knowing & Growing Chamomile

Dew-covered flower cones of German chamomile. *Susan Belsinger*

Two Herbs with the Same Name: Chamomile

Susan Belsinger & Arthur O. Tucker

The following information is excerpted from *The Culinary Herbal* by Susan Belsinger and Arthur O. Tucker, Timber Press, 2016.

German chamomile
Matricaria recutita

German chamomile, alias Hungarian chamomile, is widely confused with Roman chamomile, *Chamaemelum nobile*, and the two have been used almost interchangeably. However, Roman chamomile is a low, ground-hugging perennial while German chamomile is an upright annual, and the essential oils are also vastly different. Ingesting Roman chamomile sometimes induces allergic responses in ragweed-sensitive individuals, but such responses are rare for German chamomile.

The essential oil from German chamomile flowers has been used in nonalcoholic beverages, alcoholic beverages, ice cream and ices, candy, baked goods, and chewing gum, although the most popular use of the dried flowers seems to be in teas or tisanes. The aroma of German chamomile tea is that of daisies and fresh hay with tinges of apple. The flavor echoes the fragrance; although there is a pleasant sweetness, it is also slightly bitter. Besides having no caffeine, German chamomile tea also has health benefits. Research has shown that German chamomile reduces inflammation, allergies, and muscle spasms, and is effective against certain fungi and bacteria.

A very large number of seed lines of German chamomile have been developed, especially by the Hungarians. Some specialty catalogs will occasionally carry these, but the straight species is what we normally grow.

German Chamomile

Matricaria chamomilla L. Blackwell, E., *Herbarium Blackwellianum*, 1757.

Chamaemelum. | 1-10 Blume
11 Saame
12 Wurzel | *Samillen.*

Growing basics

annual from 3 inches to 2 feet

seedlings can withstand frost

full sun

moist, not constantly wet

well-drained garden soil; pH average 6.7

Cultivation and propagation

German chamomile grows best in a light, sandy loam with abundant moisture. Additional fertilizers should have a ratio of 1 nitrogen: 2 potassium because nitrogen delays the transition from the vegetative to the flowering stage, while potassium advances flowering. The surface of the soil should be firm to ensure good contact with the seeds in furrows 2 to 4 inches high and plants established in rows 4 to 32 inches apart.

Early autumn seeding is best in areas with regular autumn rain, late autumn seeding is best in areas with early frost and little snowfall, and spring seeding is best in areas with spring rain. Spring sowings produce a higher content of essential oils, and this is when we normally seed our German chamomile. Seeds germinate at 43 to 45°F within seven to ten days after seeding.

Leaf rosettes form thirty to forty days after germination and flowers quickly follow. Optimal temperature for flowering is 66 to 68°F. At 82 to 90°F, the flowering time is shortened.

Harvesting and preserving

Under optimal conditions, German chamomile flowers two to three times per year. Regeneration of flowers after cutting requires ten to twenty days, depending upon weather conditions. Flowers may be distilled or dried with forced hot air. The highest essential oil content is found in fully developed flowers approximately one week after beginning of flowering.

Chamaemelum Romanum. { 1–7. Blume } *Römische Chamillen*
                        { 8.9. Saame }

Roman Chamomile
Chamaemelum nobile (L.) All. Blackwell, E. *Herbarium Blackwellianum*, 1773

Roman chamomile
Chamaemelum nobile

Roman chamomile may be every herb gardener's favorite plant to simply walk on; a barefoot sunrise meander through a patch of chamomile on a dewy summer morning may bring to the body a soft tranquility and to the nose a fruity aroma reminiscent of bananas and apples when crushed. The odor has been described as sweet herbaceous, somewhat fruity-warm and tea leaf-like with nuances of green apples and bananas, while the taste has the fruity, herbaceous characteristics along with a mild bitterness.

Ingestion of raw Roman chamomile as tea, bee-pollen, and even honey can induce various allergic reactions in susceptible individuals (particularly those who are ragweed-sensitive), including skin and respiratory reactions, abdominal pain, and vomiting. Roman chamomile rinses and cosmetics may also induce localized allergic reactions in sensitive individuals, such as conjunctivitis (inflammation of mucous membranes, as around the eyelids).

The essential oil and extract of Roman chamomile is used commercially in alcoholic and non-alcoholic beverages and also finds limited use in ice cream, ices, candy, baked goods, gelatins, and puddings and provides a somewhat bitter, fruity-herbaceous warm note.

Our Picks:

At least two different cultivars are available. 'Flore Pleno' has double white flowers rising to about 3 inches. 'Treneague' generally does not flower, thus making it ideal for lawns or as a non-flowering ground cover.

Growing basics

perennial to 12 inches
hardy to zone 5
partial to full sun
moist, not constantly wet, pH average to 7.0

Cultivation and propagation

Commercial cultivation centers upon the cultivar 'Flore Pleno', and the home gardener will find this typically grows the best. However, gardeners with hot summers will find that Roman chamomile will not grow as abundantly as seen in England. Under the best circumstances, the home gardener should be happy to allow Roman chamomile to simply ramble cottage-garden style through the moist, humusy border along walking stones.

Harvesting and preserving

Flowers are harvested from late July to early August and then either dried or distilled.

Container-grown chamomiles; the shorter-growing Roman in the front and the taller German in the back. *Susan Belsinger*

Observations in Growing Both German Chamomile (*Matricaria recutita*) & Roman Chamomile (*Chamaemelum nobile*) Side by Side in my Garden

Susan Belsinger

Knowing that Chamomile was going to be Herb of the Year 2025, I decided to grow both species in my zone 7 garden alongside one another for comparison purposes. I propagated both German (*Matricaria recutita*) and Roman chamomile (*Chamaemelum nobile*) from seed purchased from Johnny's Selected Seeds, in a greenhouse with heat mats underneath the flats. I also sowed *Matricaria recutita* 'Bodegold' (John Scheeper's Kitchen Garden Seed) as well as St. John's chamomile, *Anthemis sancti-johannes* (Grand Prismatic Seed). After sowing, I left the flats in a heated greenhouse, where they were cared for—and when I returned in two weeks, all seeds had germinated.

Once the seeds were of a sturdy, transplantable size (about 6 to 8 weeks old), and the weather was warm enough, I transplanted them into the garden. I made three rows in the garden loam: back row was *Matricaria recutita* 'Bodegold', center row was German chamonile (*Matricaria recutita*) and front row was Roman chamomile (*Chamaemelum nobile*). I also planted one each of the latter two, side by side in containers.

Matricaria recutita grew taller almost immediately and the foliage was a bit more sparse on the stems compared to *Chamaemelum nobile*, which had a lower growth habit with thicker foliage on the stems. The annual *Matricaria* sent up its flower stalk before the perennial *Chamaemelum* and therefore bloomed a few weeks prior to the lower growing perennial. Flower stems for the German chamomile reached a height of about 20 to 24 inches in the height of the season, while the Roman chamomile bloomed on stems about

12 inches in height.

The flowers of German chamomile tend to have dome-shaped centers (though they vary from mounded to really dome-like) and their stems are divided like a corymb. Roman chamomile blooms tend to have flatter centers (though some are mounded domes) and the flowers are on single stems. I found that the feathery foliage and tiny blooms of both chamomiles have a pleasant applelike scent that is a tad floral, and suggests hay to my olfactory. The taste is definitely herbaceous and haylike, a bit fruity (apples and maybe even a hint of citrus) with a bitter aftertaste. When dried these characteristics are more concentrated.

I harvested flowers daily—or every other day—like you have to do for calendula since they do not open all at once and keep producing blooms. I definitely got a higher yield of flowers from the *Matricaria recutita*. Once it got hot in August the plants really slowed down production of leaf and flower. The plants in containers did not grow as large or bloom as prolifically as the ones in the garden earth.

I look forward to next season—to see if the annual *Matricaria recutita* dropped seed and will give me volunteer plants—and if the perennial *Chamaemelum nobile* will return where it was planted. The information herein is from my own personal experience and observations.

Susan Belsinger bio on page 17.

Chamomile seedlings being planted out in the garden. *Susan Belsinger*

A Few Chamomile Relatives that I Have Met

Susan Belsinger

In researching and studying the chamomiles, I came across different genuses, species within the genus and plants called chamomile, that are not really chamomile. I would like to mention a few of them here briefly because they relate to *Matricaria recutita* (syn. *M. chamomilla*), commonly referred to as the annual German chamomile, or *Chamaemelum nobile* (formerly *Anthemis nobilis*), the perennial Roman chamomile, in some way and I feel are worth noting. All of these botanicals belong to the Asteraceae family.

Matricaria discoidea is known as **pineapple weed** and smells quite a lot like the tropical fruit pineapple. If you are uncertain when identifying this plant, all you have to do is use your nose to identify its fruity fragrance which is surprisingly pineapple-like. Another identifying characteristic to this low-growing herb is the flowers. The blooms are borne on feathery foliage that looks like other chamomiles, except that it is thick and dense and the bloom stems are short and stay close to the foliage. The flowers are primarily composed of a center disk which is domed, greenish yellow in color and there are no flower petals.

My neighbors at Sharp Farm here in Brookeville, Maryland, have a field of it, which I have laid down in and observed the growth closely—as well as the pineapple scent—and abuzz with pollinators. It doesn't get much taller than 6 to 8 inches in height even with the bloom stalk. It seems to grow in anthropogenic places (soils that have been disturbed—rather like plantain—known as "white man's footsteps").

Originally native to North America, pineapple weed has naturalized in Europe and Eurasia. Upon tasting it—it is a bit fruity (though not as pineapple-like as it smells), herbaceous with a slightly bitter aftertaste. I have made a tisane with it and added it to lemonade. I imagine it could be successfully made into a sorbet or ice cream. I haven't tried a syrup, however I am sure it would be good in a mock or cocktail with some mineral water or seltzer.

Medicinally its virtues are more similar to German chamomile (*M. chamaemelum*)—even more so than Roman chamomile. It helps with digestive tract issues, stomachache and cramps and is relaxing taken as a tisane or used in the bath.

Pineapple weed growing wild near Brookeville, Maryland. *Susan Belsinger*

Cota tinctoria syn. *Anthemis tinctoria,* whose common name is **dyer's chamomile** or golden Marguerite, is also sometimes called yellow chamomile due to its bright golden yellow flowers which are used as a dye plant. The flowers, used fresh or dried, yield a bright yellow dye, while the leaves produce a light green hue. This plant is highly regarded by those who use dye plants as being one of the best yellow dyes. Native to Europe, dyers' chamomile has naturalized to many parts of the United States. It is also called oxeye chamomile and Boston or Paris daisy.

Plants reach about 2 feet in height when flowering. Although this plant is a perennial, Farmacie Isolde, who sells the seed, recommends sowing it every year like an annual and planting it in the garden to aid in growing vegetables. They also use it to make a botanical tea: "This chamomile may be used in combination with Yarrow and Nettles to create a fantastic biodynamic fertilizer: steep foliage for a week or more in a bucket of clean water outdoors in full sun. May be diluted further and used to water vegetable species as necessary."

The flowers can be made into a tea though it does not have the same medicinal virtues as German and Roman chamomile.

Dyer's chamomile, grown from seed. Heritage Herb Garden, Ozark Folk Center State Park, Mountain View, Arkansas. *Susan Belsinger*

Anthemis cotula syn. *A. foetida*, *Maruta cotula, is* also known as **stinking chamomile**, mayweed, stinkweed and dog fennel. Always on the lookout for the upcoming herbs of the year, I was so excited to find this lovely chamomile plant growing wild when I went to visit my daughter Lucie and her husband Matt on their organic farm in southwest Oregon. That is until I bent down to rub and smell it—it took me aback at how stinky it was—and it didn't taste any better than it smelled! Visually it looks very much like German chamomile, however that is where the similarities stop; the odor is rank and it has an acrid taste. Plants for a Future.org website states: "Easily confused with *A. arvensis* but its strong smell gives it away."

Native to Eurasia, stinking chamomile is considered a noxious weed in some parts of the U.S. where it has naturalized. It is another anthropogenic plant which appears in disturbed soils and can grow anywhere from 8 to over 24 inches in height. According to ediblewildfoods.com: "This wild plant is not a commonly sought-after edible for foragers and for good reason. Caution is advised with this plant. Very small quantities of the leaves can be used as a flavouring herb and the flowers can be used to make a tea but they are much weaker than chamomile for its calming effects."

This stinking chamomile photo was taken at Harbinger Farm (growing wild) in Myrtle Creek, Oregon. *Susan Belsinger*

References

https://www.bbg.org/article/weed_of_the_month_pineapple_weed. Accessed June 15, 2024

https://www.farmacieisolde.com/tinctoria/dyers-chamomile. Accessed November 1, 2024

https://gobotany.nativeplanttrust.org/species/anthemis/cotula/. Accessed November 1, 2024

https://www.ediblewildfood.com/stinking-chamomile.aspx. Accessed November 1, 2024

https://www.minnesotawildflowers.info/flower/dog-fennel. Accessed November 1, 2024

https://pfaf.org/user/Plant.aspx?LatinName=Anthemis+cotula. Accessed November 1, 2024

Although **Susan Belsinger** celebrated and gave programs for the International Herb Association's Herb of the Year selections since the program first began in 1995, she first began contributing to the booklets in 2006. She joined Chuck Voigt as co-editor of *Scented Geraniums, Herb of the Year 2006* and *Lemon Balm, Herb of the Year 2007*, expanding them to 70 pages with black and white photographs. In 2007, Susan took over as editor and IHA published their first bound book of nearly 100 pages with color cover, *Calendula, Herb of the Year 2008*. She was editor for *Bay, Herb of the Year 2009* (first color insert); *Dill, Herb of the Year 2010*; *Horseradish, Herb of the Year 2011* and *Rose, Herb of the Year, 2012* (expanded to 260 pages).

Since then, Susan has contributed articles, poems, photographs and proofread each HOY book to date. Susan delights in each new Herb of the Year: doing research, growing the specimens, taking photos, creating recipes and herbal formulations, sharing her findings and celebrating the plants. She was the Otto Richter Award recipient in 2009 and received the IHA award for Outstanding Contributions to the Herb Industry in 2004 and served on the IHA board from 2005 to 2010.

www.susanbelsinger.com

https://www.instagram.com/cookinwithherbs/

https://www.facebook.com/susan.belsinger

https://www.facebook.com/CreativeHerbalHome

Pineapple weed, *Matricaria discoidea. www.commons.wikimedia.org*

Chamomile Weeds

Kathleen Connole

Pineapple weed, *Matricaria discoidea* and stinking chamomile, *Anthemis cotula* L. are both common to North America as well as Europe and Eurasia. There is some debate as to the native origin of pineapple weed. The Plants of the World Online database, Kew, states that its range is Subarctic America to the United States, primarily in the temperate biome (www.kew.org); and that is has been introduced into northern Europe, Eurasia, and Australia. The Native Plant Trust, *Hortus III* and *The Flora of North America* agree with Kew.

The spread of the fruitily perfumed pineapple weed, which arrived in Britain from Oregon in 1871, exactly tracked the adoption of the treaded motor tyre, to which its ribbed seeds clung as if they were the soles of small climbing boots. – Richard Mabey, Weeds: In Defense of Nature's Most Unloved Plants

The chamomiles are members of the Asteraceae family, which contains some 23,000 species, and today this plant family is found on every continent on earth except Antarctica. The oldest pollen samples of Asteraceae to date have been found in Patagonia, dating back 65 to 50 million years ago, when this now subarctic region was home to tropical forests. Patagonia, New Zealand, Australia, and Antarctica, which are in the world's highest latitudes in the southern hemisphere, and were once interconnected, witnessed the early evolution of this plant family.

Asteraceae is the most diverse group within the angiosperms, the flowering plants. Characteristics such as a relatively short generation time, rapid population growth, and the close association with insect pollinators gave these plants an adaptive advantage over the more ancient gymnosperms. The family Asteraceae was and is of major influence in "the diversification and evolution of a large numbers of animals that rely on their inflorescences to survive" (Barreda, www.doi.org). (Including humans.) The most recent common ancestors of this plant family were present in the land mass called

Gondwana 80 million years ago. During the late Paleocene and early Eocene, 60 to 50 million years ago, as the climate warmed, there was a dramatic rise in the diversity of flowering plants. It was during this epoch that the continents drifted apart, so, it makes sense that plant families that were once connected came to be separated by the oceans.

Recent scientific analysis of the chlorotype lineages of German chamomile, *Matricaria recutita,* and pineapple weed, *Matricaria discoidea,* reveal that these two species are more closely related than any others in the genus and have a common ancestor (Ruzicka, et al, 2024).

Pineapple weed was one of the plants collected by the Lewis and Clark Expedition. Meriwether Lewis collected it on the Weippe Prairie in Clearwater County, Idaho, on 12 June 1806. Plant explorer Thomas Nuttall grew pineapple weed from seeds collected; this is believed to be the actual herbarium specimen in the Lewis and Clark plant collection. The authors of *Lewis and Clark's Green World*, Scott Earle and James Reveal, write, regarding the pineapple weed herbarium specimen in the collection: "There is nothing in the expedition's journals about the plant, but it would seem that there was little reason for Lewis to collect the two specimens that he brought back other than for its agreeable sweet scent."

The Native American Ethnobotany Database is the result of over 25 years of research. It lists 4,029 species from 243 plant families and more than 44,000 uses by 291 Native American groups. Approximately one half of the uses listed are medicinal; the other uses include food, dyes, fiber, fragrance, and ceremonial. The project began in the 1970s with around 1,000 listings on punch-edge index cards. As more data was collected this system became "very unwieldy." The next step was to transfer the information to the University of Michigan's mainframe computer; the software used was one of the first database management systems. In 1977 *Native American Ethnobotany* by Daniel E. Moerman was published, describing 4,869 items (naeb.brit.org). Today the entire database is online and is very useful for researching the uses of plants by native peoples of North America.

Pineapple weed, *Matricaria discoidea,* and stinking chamomile, *Anthemis cotula,* are both listed in the NAEB Database.

Most of the native peoples documented to make use of pineapple weed inhabited areas of northern North America: the Aleut, Blackfoot, Cahuilla, Cheyenne, Costanoan, Crow, Dregueno, Flathead, Inuit, Kutenai, Montana,

Okanagan-Coville, Shuswap, Ute, and Yokia. It also is listed as being used by the Cherokee people of the eastern woodlands.

The most common uses were infusions or decoctions of leaves and flowers, as analgesic; there were many gastrointestinal applications including as carminative, laxative, antidiarrheal, for colic; as a dermatological aid and febrifuge; gynecological uses for menstrual cramps and as an aid during and after childbirth; to treat children's colds and convulsions; as a "panacea and cure-all."

The crushed dried seeds were used in a salve to treat infected sores, and as a decoction for colds and indigestion. Fiber from the plant was used for mats, rugs, bedding, and to line baby cradles.

The dried plant was pulverized and used to keep insects away from preserved meat and berries. The bloom time of pineapple weed was used as an indicator that it was time to harvest salmonberries. Children enjoyed eating the fresh flower heads.

The aromatic quality of pineapple weed made it a popular choice for perfume, incense for steam baths, sweat lodges, and ceremonies including the Sun Dance. This plant was also used as part of a "love medicine"—the tops were buried with human hair to prevent loved ones or relations from going away; or with horsehair to prevent horses from running away.

Our forager friend and author Bo Brown advises that the young leaves and flowers of pineapple weed can be enjoyed in green salads and add flavor to cooked dishes. He recommends a tea made from the green or dried leaves for diarrhea and stomach pain (Brown, p.58).

Another chamomile relative, the weed known as stinking chamomile, *Anthemis cotula* is considered to be native to Europe and Eurasia, and introduced into North America. It is listed in the NAEB database as being used by the Cherokee, Iroquois, Karok, Mendicino, Mohegan, and Yuki people.

All parts of the plant were used: often as a decoction, sometimes as a cold infusion for "spring fever or summer complaint." The many medicinal uses listed include as analgesic, antidiarrheal, anticonvulsive, antirheumatic, blood purifier, dermatological aid, diaphoretic, emetic, febrifuge; gynecological, kidney, pediatric, and respiratory aid; sedative, venereal treatment, and as a panacea or tonic "to benefit the entire body." The root was chewed for toothache.

From *Weeds and What They Tell* (ed. 1970) by Ehrenfried Pfeiffer:

Weeds are WEEDS only from our human egotistical point of view, because they grow where we do not want them. In Nature, however, they play an important and interesting role. They resist conditions which cultivated plants cannot resist, such as drought, acidity of soil, lack of humus, mineral deficiencies, as well as a one-sidedness of minerals, etc. They are witness of [humanity's] failure to master the soil, and they grow abundantly wherever [humans] have 'missed the train' – they only indicate our errors and Nature's corrections. Weeds want to tell a story – they are nature's way of teaching [us] – and their story is interesting. If we would only listen to it we could apprehend a great deal of the finer forces through which Nature helps and heals and balances and, sometimes, also has fun with us.

Or, as my favorite University of Missouri Professor of Horticulture, Dr. David Trinklein, always said, "A weed is just a plant out of place."

References

Brown, Bo. *Foraging Central Grasslands*. The Rowman and Littlefield Publishing Group, Inc., 2023.

Earle, S. and J. Reveal. *Lewis and Clark's Green World*. Farcountry Press, 2003.

Pfeiffer, E. *Weeds and What They Tell*. Floris Books, 2012.

Chamomile. www.naeb.brit.org/uses/search/?string=Matricaria. Accessed 11-11-24.

Mabey, R. *Weeds: In Defense of Nature's Most Unloved Plants*. Ecco, 2012.

Matricaria discoidea. www.betafloranorthamerica.org/matricaria_discoidea. Accessed 11-11-24.

Matricaria discoidea. www.gobotany.nativeplanttrust.org/species/matricaria/discoidea/. Accessed 11-11-24.

Matricaria. www.naeb.brit.org/uses/search/?string=Matricaria. Accessed 11-11-24.

Matricaria discoidea. www.powo.science.kew.org/taxon/um:lsid:ipni.org:1547162. Accessed 11-11-24.

Kathleen Connole joined the Ozark Folk Center's Heritage Herb Garden team in 2006. Before moving to Arkansas' Buffalo River Country in 2005, Kathleen earned a degree in Plant Science from the University of Missouri-Columbia and worked at Powell Gardens and Farrand Farms in Kansas City, Missouri. Kathleen researches the natural history of the Heritage Herb Garden's diverse herbal collection and composes interpretive signage for the Garden to tell the stories of these plants. After spending several years recovering from major surgeries, she is thrilled to once again be able to hike the hills and hollows of the Ozarks, botanizing while in search of waterfalls and spectacular view spots. Kathleen served as chair and is an active member of the Herb Society of America Ozark Unit, headquartered at the Ozark Folk Center State Park. She currently is secretary for the International Herb Association Board. She was editor of the IHA's *Viola Herb of the Year 2022*, *Ginger Herb of the Year 2023*, *Yarrow Herb of the Year 2024*, and is currently editor of *Chamomile Herb of the Year 2025*.

Stinking chamomile can be found growing in disturbed sites.
Susan Belsinger

Courageous, Compassionate Chamomile

Rosemary Roman Davis

Chamomile and Camomile

If you pronounce it Chamomile
That will your Yankiness reveal
For Brits assume it more worthwhile
To render it as Camomile

So wear a wreath of Chamomile
To make your beauty sweeter still,
Then pour some tea with Camomile
To have your lunch in British style

---Artyom Timeyev
All Poetry, 2017

Chamomile, native to Europe and Asia, has multiple identities: there are over 20 species worldwide, and many hybrids are bred specifically for their looks, their chemical content, or their growing habits. The botanical nomenclature can be confusing depending on the printed source consulted by the gardener; our discourse here will apply, except where noted, to either German chamomile (*Matricaria chamomilla* or *M. recutita*), an annual herb, or Roman chamomile (*Chamaemelum nobile* or *Anthemis nobilis*), which is perennial.

When Carl Linnaeus devised his binomial method of classifying and identifying plants in the eighteenth century, he created a system of nomenclature which drew on the commonly accepted scientific practice of the time: combining sensibly descriptive words drawn from both Greek and Latin. These classical languages, commonly understood by the educated people of his era, allowed botanists and gardeners to communicate with each other concerning the identities and properties of useful plants. It is undeniable that both languages yielded colorful and often poetic names which remain with us to this day.

Matricaria derives from the Latin root for "mother/matrix/womb/that which generates". *Chamomilla* stems from the Greek χαμαί ("on the ground") and μήλον ("apple".) This is neatly translated into one of chamomile's numerous folk names, "ground-apple." The apple references in chamomile's history point to its light yet distinctive fruity scent. *Recutita* translates as "lacking an epidermis" or in some translations, "circumcised." *Nobilis* means elevated or noble, well known. Other folk names for chamomile are mayweed, whig plant, and maythen.

Having got the morphology out of the way, let us plunge into the properties of this amazingly edible, medicinal and ornamental plant ally!

Meet The Relatives

Chamomile's family picnic of indirect relations could include some of the following guests:

Dyer's chamomile (*Anthemis tinctoria* or *Cota tinctoria*). Also known as ox-eye chamomile and golden Marguerite. Native to Europe, Iran and the Caucasus, it yields a yellow, khaki or olive dye depending on the mordant used. However, even common chamomiles can be used to produce yellow or gray-green dyes using the flowers, and light to bright green dye using just the leaves and stems.

Moroccan chamomile (*Chamaemelum mixtum* or *Cladanthus mixtus*). An annual, not a true chamomile. It shares some medicinal qualities with chamomile, but its essential oil is most commonly used in the perfume industry.

Wild chamomile (*Matricaria discoidea*). Also known as pineapple-weed for its somewhat stronger fruity fragrance when crushed. Native to North America, it shares many of chamomile's healing abilities and was used by the indigenous American tribes. It has stronger vulnerary qualities than German or Roman chamomile.

The Travel Miles of Chamomile

In history, folklore, and magical use, chamomile makes its appearance in ancient Egypt, Greece and Rome. The Egyptians, taking their cue from the flower's shape, classified it as a solar herb and dedicated it to the god Ra. Medicinally, it was used primarily in Egypt for malaria, and was also included in mummification rituals.

Nicholas Culpeper, naturally, had to weigh in on chamomile. He recommended it for everything from fevers to melancholy, colic, dropsy, indigestion, and jaundice, but was quite sour about the Egyptians, stating that "they dedicated it to the Sun because it cured agues. They were like enough to do that for they were the arrantest apes in their religion I ever read of."

However, he continues, "It is profitable for melancholy or for an inflammation of the bowels and there is nothing more profitable than to apply it to the sides and region of the liver and spleen." John Gerard cited it as a helpful emmenagogue and treatment for kidney stones.

One variety grows wild in the Middle East where its common name is "dog chamomile"—because its sometimes musky smell is thought to resemble that of an unkempt dogs' kennel. It is thought to be a plant possibly linked to the Biblical reference regarding the "lilies of the field" (Matthew 6:28). Being an annual in that part of the world, it could be interpreted not literally as a tropical or subtropical lily (scholars believe that other native flowers would be the basis for this quote from the Sermon on the Mount) but as a symbol of the impermanence and frailty of human life.

Chamomile is the national herb of Russia, and has a long history of use there as both food and medicine. It is also a traditional addition to funeral wreaths. Both Avicenna (Ibn Sina) and Dioscorides mention chamomile as a healing herb; Dioscorides recommends it as a febrifuge in his writings of 900 BCE. Avicenna recommends it as a relaxant and an anti-inflammatory herb, used both internally and externally. As with many other fragrant plants, chamomile was, and is, an easily available and lovely plant to use as both a household strewing herb to repel insects, and a plant called upon for purifying and sanctifying burial rituals.

Chamomile is one of the nine sacred herbs of the Saxons (the others, should you be curious, are mugwort, plantain, lamb's cress, fumitory, nettle, crab apple, chervil, and fennel). We are not quite sure who first transcribed the poetic charm citing these healing plants dating from the tenth or eleventh century, but all the plants included are nutritious, medicinal, and still used today for the same purposes the Saxons recorded. All nine are included in the recipe for a healing salve which concludes the text, which appears to be a cure-all remedy for rashes, wounds, and swellings.

The Benedictine Order included chamomile in its alcoholic formulations, and it is still an ingredient in some brands of vermouth and absinthe. Viewed as a lucky herb which attracts money, it is folk wisdom for gamblers to wash their hands in a solution of chamomile before gaming or betting.

Chemical Composition and Usage

Our courageous green friend looks innocent, yet contains a positive buffet of over 100 chemical components: flavonoids, apigenin (which slows brain activity), glycosides, terpines (anti-inflammatory compounds which slow down cytokine production), fatty acids, salicylate derivatives, tannins, and chamazulene (which gives its distinctive bright blue color to German chamomile essential oil, the most common type for cosmetic use).

In comparing German chamomile to Roman, their chemical components are similar but not identical. The chemicals in German chamomile are primarily terpenoids, while Roman chamomile contains more acids and acid esters. German chamomile essential oil contains approximately 50% chamazulenes, hence its deep azure color; Roman chamomile essential oil is a much lighter blue and oxidizes quickly to a light yellow, possessing only 5% chamazulene content.

With so much packed into one unassuming herb, for what does one use it? The courageous magic of chamomile lies in its synergistic power; like most herbs, its chemical components, if separated, would be far less useful if they were not accessed using the whole plant. In 2000 the USDA approved chamomile as GRAS (generally regarded as safe) for use in over-the-counter dietary supplements.

Chamomile is best known as a general calming and carminative agent. Most of us first read of this when Peter Rabbit's mother put him to bed with chamomile tea after his bilious eating spree in Mr. McGregor's garden. As a calming agent suitable and safe even for children, chamomile is peerless. It is mildly sedative, digestive, anti-inflammatory, antidepressant, antiseptic, nervine, vulnerary, antispasmodic, anthelmintic, diaphoretic, and antibiotic.

Unlike many other herbs, its gentle assistance is immediate; it is not necessary to apply or consume the herb for weeks or months for a cumulative effect.

The carminative/digestive powers of chamomile are tempered by the advice of Dr. Robert Thornton, who wrote an herbal in the early 19th century praising but rebuking chamomile. Originally destined for the clergy, Dr. Thornton switched tracks and became both a botanist and a physician while studying at Cambridge. Regarding chamomile, he wrote:

Although this be a fine remedy, and merits all our praise, still it must be remembered, that as the cord too tightly strung, relaxes its tone, so as never to recover again, thus the stomach, too much braced by a long-continued use of camomile tea, loses irrecoverably its tone, and becomes a truly afflicting evil arising from imprudent use of this tonic.

Dr. Thornton makes a very modern point, in that overuse of any substance, no matter how dulcet, is usually a bad idea, as it probably conceals a larger underlying issue. And indeed, the chemical components in chamomile do act directly on smooth (stomach) muscle. It might be posited that overuse of a gastric relaxant could indeed interfere with one's ability to digest food properly over time.

However, let's add one of his prescriptions here, which sounds quite delightful even if you are not bilious or dyspeptic:

Rx.3

Take of camomile flowers

Lemon peel

Orange peel, of each drachms 4

Boiling water 1 pint

Let them remain for four hours, and strain. To the strained liquor add syrup of ginger, drachms 6. The dose is a wine glass in the morning early, and repeated an hour before dinner, for habits debilitated by drinking, or natural weakness of the stomach.

This recipe is rather more vigorous:

Rx.4

Take of camomile flowers drachms 3

Rhubarb, in powder, drachms 2

Coriander seeds bruised, drachms 1

Make into tea, by adding a quart of boiling water over night. A wine glass is to be taken half an hour before dinner to create an appetite.

Save this one for the day before Thanksgiving, perhaps.

This amazing herb plays well with others, too; its components show a remarkable ability to engage in synergy with other beneficial plants with low instances of contraindication. In its soothing and digestive role, it works well on its own, but even better with mint, ginger and fennel. As a tea for nervous overstimulation and anxiety, it can be combined with catnip, skullcap or valerian. When fighting off a urinary tract imbalance, it blends well with corn silk, plantain, and marshmallow. Chamomile may be fermented into an ale like many other herbs and is reputed to magnify and enhance the intoxicating qualities of psychotropic herbs used in brewing.

Although some individuals may display a sensitivity to chamomile if they are allergic to other herbal cousins (Asteraceae family, such as ragweed, daisies, marigold, and chrysanthemum)—oddly enough, chamomile is also a remedy for other allergy sufferers, who may use the herb to boost their systems against environmental irritants. The plant components typically used are the leaves, flowers, and stems, either infused or tinctured; the essential oil may be included in lotions, creams or balms.

Cosmetically, chamomile infusion is a skin-friendly wash for irritated or acne-prone skin, and a pleasant balancing rinse for any hair type. The flowers have frequently been used as a brightening hair rinse for blonde hair, although they will also impart slight highlights to dark hair with repeated use. It's recommended to combine additional botanicals such as calendula or henna with chamomile if actual color change is desired. The herbal infusion, used liberally as either a drenching solution or poultice, is also recommended for conjunctivitis, general eye irritation, eczema, and gum disease.

For skin irritations, a potent topical remedy can be created by adding chamomile essential oil or tincture to a neutral (unscented) cream or lotion of your choice. It has been noted as a soothing and healing demulcent for irradiated skin during cancer treatment. Animal studies have shown that chamomile may have anti-ulcer and anti-tumor potential.

Chamomile is available as a homeopathic remedy (which may be labeled "Chamomilla"). It is specific for nervous emotional conditions, insomnia, drug withdrawal, diverticulosis, and particularly for teething problems, in both small humans and puppies who are in the endless-chewing-gnawing-drooling stage. Chamomile is especially beloved for use with children as it is so gentle, and targets both the digestive and emotional complaints common to youngsters. In addition, it is a steadfast remedy for the many and varied physical complaints common to pregnancy and the menstrual cycle.

Given that our modern culture is presenting more and more individuals who suffer from ADHD, autism, and other neurodivergent challenges, the smelling salt recipe given at the end of this essay is a small but helpful weapon against the hurdles they face. Useful for everyone, of course; but especially for a child suffering from worries about testing at school, social anxiety, overstimulation, trouble sleeping, trouble focusing—chamomile can lend a helping hand in all these situations.

For use in farm and stable, bunches of chamomile hung in the barn have long been used as a fly repellent. Used as an infusion or a poultice, both pets and farm animals respond to the gentle effects of chamomile for eye inflammation, gum disease, and skin irritations. A strong tea of the flowers is helpful as a blood cleanser and restorative for all livestock during postpartum recovery.

Chamomile In Garden Design

Falstaff speaks to us of chamomile in Shakespeare's play *Henry IV*, Part I (Act II, Scene IV):

Peace, good pint-pot; peace, good tickle-brain. Harry, I do not only marvel where thou spendest thy time, but also how thou art accompanied: for though the camomile, the more it is trodden on, the faster it grows, yet youth, the more it is wasted, the sooner it wears.

Here, Falstaff is impersonating Prince Harry's father, the King. He jests in acting out the first-class scolding that he imagines Harry is about to receive when he returns to court at his father's command; Harry will be expected to explain why exactly he has been wasting his formative years hanging about in taverns with scoundrelly knaves such as Falstaff, instead of being a responsible heir to the throne.

In this passage, we are seeing a reference to Roman chamomile, the low-growing and patient variety which was indeed greatly favored in England in the Tudor era for lawns, garden seats crafted out of turf blocks, and herbal borders. Maud Grieve paraphrases Shakespeare in her *Modern Herbal*, citing the herb's reputation to release scent when walked upon. Low-growing, drought tolerant, durable and fragrant when trodden or bruised, it became quite fashionable as a ground cover which did not need to be mowed or shorn—something many gardeners are prudently reviving today. The modern variant named 'Treneague', a non-flowering chamomile, is a common hybrid for usage as a lawn. 'Flore Pleno' is a double-flowered variety which also remains short in stature.

In more modern times, chamomile has even become popular as a planting for cricket pitches, although for players who are allergic to this plant family that might not be a favorable idea! It is worth noting that exposure of this nature would more than likely be troublesome due to chamomile's pollen, meaning that sensitive individuals would probably be able to use chamomile for physical complaints in tincture or oil form without ill effects. Indeed, it is said that, of old, consumptives would be ordered to sit next to beds of chamomile, breathing in the fragrance of the plants in order to ease their pulmonary distress.

If they were consumptive *and* allergic, and also played cricket—well, that probably didn't end on a positive note. But that's not chamomile's fault.

Roman chamomile is indeed a friend of the herbaceous border, and forms a comely pathway in place of stone or gravel, rarely growing more than four inches in height. German chamomile, a taller, more feathery, droopy herb which can reach two feet in height, looks well when planted in contrast to broad-leaved plants such as borage, comfrey, and elecampane. Roman chamomile is perennial and spreads via runners, whereas German chamomile is a self-seeding annual. Both exist in USDA zones 4 to 11 and are not terribly fussy about sun or part shade; they are quite drought tolerant and are not easily troubled by insect pests. As with most herbs, drier, slightly sandy ground will yield happier plants with stronger essential oil content than those grown in more soggy earth. Henry Beston recommended Roman chamomile especially for rock gardens and also, amusingly, as "a relief from Sedums."

Chamomile is known to benefit ailing plants growing nearby, and is even credited with reviving tired cut flowers in the vase. Planted as a neighbor, it repels cabbage moths and worms from all vegetables in the *Brassica* family and attracts ladybugs and beneficial wasps. Medieval gardeners included chamomile in their patterned physic knot-gardens, in the company of other sedative and antispasmodic herbs such as catnip, dill, hops, lemon balm, skullcap, and valerian.

In Thomas Jefferson's garden log of 1793, we see that chamomile was included in the many and varied garden beds situated around the estate of Monticello. German chamomile is commercially cultivated worldwide, in Egypt, Russia, Bulgaria, Hungary and Germany.

It is not recommended to plant parsley, carrots, parsnips, and particularly mint, near chamomile (as the two would combat each other in producing their unique essential oils).

Esoteric Use

This applies to either type of chamomile essential oil.

Versatile chamomile is known as an herb of purification, protection, and good luck. It is linked not only to Ra, but to all solar deities such as Lugh, Helios, and Cernunnos. As such, it is planted to guard the home, used in incense, worn or carried for good luck, used to attract both love and money, and sprinkled around one's property to repel negative forces.

Planted on a grave, it is said to ensure restful peace for the departed and to ease their transition from this world. Hung over a crib, it is said to protect infants.

Chamomile is an unassuming plant with truly awesome powers. Easily grown and widely available, we should give thanks for the restorative, soothing, and healing qualities of this singular centuries-old plant ally!

I hope you will make room in your garden for this humble, cheerful and courageous herb.

Happy Gardening and Blessed Be!

Emotional Rescue Smelling Salts

Fill a one-ounce glass container, preferably dark-colored, with coarse kosher salt or coarse sea salt. Do not use plastic bottles; pure essential oils can dissolve them quite easily.

Add ten drops chamomile essential oil, ten drops lavender essential oil, and ten drops rosemary essential oil to the salt. *Please note that it is crucial to use pure essential oils. Do not use any product marked or sold as a "fragrance oil" or "perfume oil" as these are usually synthetic.*

Citrus oils might seem a logical addition here, but popular usage suggests that citrus oils interact poorly with chamomile oil and may possibly cancel out each others' beneficial properties.

Cap the bottle tightly, shake well, and let sit overnight. Carry the bottle in backpack or purse; uncap and sniff briefly when stress or overwhelm strikes, or when mental focus is needed. Empty, clean, and refill the bottle when the scent of the essential oils has dissipated.

References

Applewood Books. *The Floral Birthday Book: Flowers and their Emblems.* Applewood Books, 2003.

Balch, James F., M.D. and Stengler, Mark, M.D. *Prescription for Natural Cures.* John Wiley & Sons, Inc., 2004.

---, and Balch, Phyllis A., CNC. *Prescription for Nutritional Healing.* Avery Publishing Group, Inc., 1990.

Beith, Mary. *Healing Threads: Traditional Medicines of the Highlands and Islands.* Edinburgh, Scotland: Polygon, 1995.

Beston, Henry. *Herbs and the Earth.* David R. Godine, Publisher, 1990.

Bremness, Lesley. *Herbs.* DK Publishing, Inc., 1994.

Buhner, Stephen Harrod. *Sacred and Herbal Healing Beers: The Secrets of Ancient Fermentation.* Siris Books, 1998.

Castleman, Michael. *The Healing Herbs.* Rodale Press, 1991.

Cox, Janice. *Natural Beauty for All Seasons.* Henry Holt and Company, Inc., 1996.

Culpeper, Nicholas. *Culpeper's Color Herbal.* Sterling Publishing

Company, Inc., 1983.

Cunningham, Scott. *Cunningham's Encyclopedia of Magical Herbs*. Llewellyn Worldwide, Ltd.: 1985.

de Baïracli Levy, Juliette. *The Complete Herbal Handbook for Farm and Stable*. London, United Kingdom: Faber and Faber Ltd., 1991.

Duerr, Sasha. *The Handbook of Natural Plant Dyes*. Timber Press, Inc., 2010.

Duke, James A., Ph.D. *A Field Guide to Medicinal Plants: Eastern and Central North America*. Rodale Press, 1987.

--- . *The Green Pharmacy*. Rodale Press, 1997.

Fougère, Barbara, BVSc. *The Pet Lover's Guide to Natural Healing for Cats & Dogs*. Elsevier Saunders, 2006.

Frazier, Anitra. *The Natural Cat*. Penguin Group, 2008.

Gerard, John. *The Herball or Generall Historie of Plantes*. London, United Kingdom: John Norton, 1597.

Grieve, Mrs. Maud. *A Modern Herbal in Two Volumes*; Vol. II: I-Z. Dover Publications, 1971.

Hoffman, David. *The New Holistic Herbal*. Element Books, Inc., 1992.

Illes, Judika. *The Encyclopedia of 5,000 Spells*. HarperCollins, 2008.

Jackson, Mildred, N.D. and Teague, Terri, N.D. *The Handbook of Alternatives to Chemical Medicine*. Coconino County, 1975.

Keville, Kathi. *Herbs: An Illustrated Encyclopedia*. Michael Friedman Publishing, Inc., 1994.

Leighton, Ann. *American Gardens in the Eighteenth Century: "For Use or For Delight"*. Houghton Mifflin Company, 1976.

Mason, Catherine. *Making An Herb Garden*. Trafalgar Square Publishing, 1997.

Massachusetts Historical Society
https://www.masshist.org/thomasjeffersonpapers/doc?id=garden_28

McIntyre, Anne. *The Medicinal Garden*. Henry Holt and Company, Inc., 1997.

Neal, Bill. *Gardener's Latin*. Algonquin Books, 1992.

Personal notes, Proceedings of the International Herb Symposium, Norton, MA, 2000-2013.

Pond, Barbara. *A Sampler of Wayside Herbs*. Greenwich House, 1974.

Robinson, Sarah. *Kitchen Witch: Food, Folklore & Fairy Tale*. Cork, Ireland, United Kingdom: Womancraft Publishing, 2022.

Rose, Jeanne. *The Herbal Body Book*. Perigee Books, 1976.

---. *375 Essential Oils and Hydrosols*. Frog, Ltd., 1999.

Seymour, Miranda. *A Brief History of Thyme and other herbs*. Grove Press, 2002.

Tilford, Gregory L. and Wulff-Tilford, Mary. *All You Ever Wanted To Know About Herbs for Pets*. Bowtie Press, 1999.

Timeyev, Artyom. https://allpoetry.com/poem/13520935-Chamomile-and-Chamomile-by-Artyom-Timeyev. Accessed 7-26-24.

Tiwari, Maya. *Ayurveda: A Life of Balance*. Healing Arts Press, 1995.

Tourles, Stephanie. *The Herbal Body Book: A Natural Approach to Healthier Hair, Skin and Nails*. Storey Communications, Inc., 1995.

---. *Herbal Home Spa: A Natural Approach to Beautiful Hair, Skin, Nails and Feet*. Thunder Bay Press, 2002.

Wigington, Patti. "Chamomile." Learn Religions, Aug. 27, 2020, learnreligions.com/chamomile-2562019.

Rosemary Roman Davis was raised in a family of herbalists and green thumbs and maintains a messy but vibrant organic garden in upstate New York. One of her first paid jobs as a high school student was office assistant at the Herb Society of America, long ago when its headquarters were located in Concord, MA! When not finding new excuses to avoid weeding, and planning for the next big endeavor—beekeeping—she is a licensed massage therapist and Reiki Master. She has also been an adult education teacher for over fifteen years, offering food folklore classes and many hands-on workshops including soapmaking, cheesemaking and papermaking.

The taller blooms of German chamomile stand out against a blue sky.

Pineapple weed, *Matricaria discoidea*, can be found happily growing in disturbed sites, parking lots, and waste places. *www.commons.wikimedia.org*

Chamomile Memories

Karen England

I have lived in North County San Diego for over fifty-five years, since I was ten years old, and as a youngster I first encountered chamomile growing in various dirt parking lots around the coastal areas of my home, school, church and work (yes, I worked for the family plant nursery from a very young age). I never thought to ask myself or anyone else, "Where did the chamomile come from?" As far as I was concerned it was just there.

In its heyday Encinitas, my hometown, was known as "The Flower Capital of the World," and a fleeting thought occurred to me that maybe chamomile was one of those capital flowers? It wasn't.

As a teenager I would walk barefoot to Moonlight Beach along Encinitas Boulevard, taking a shortcut through a dirt parking lot at the beach; there I would step on little scraggly green patches with tiny yellow flowers, and up

Pineapple weed blooms are chamomile/pineapple-scented and lack ray florets. *www.commons.wikimedia.org*

Peter helping himself to Mr. McGregor's carrots. Beatrix Potter
www.projectgutenberg.org

would come wafting the unmistakable smell of the tea that Peter Rabbit's mother served him after gorging on too many lettuces in Mr. McGregor's garden.

Mothers the world over, including my own, serve their children chamomile tea to settle an upset tummy.

Encinitas, where I lived for thirty years before moving a couple miles inland to Vista where I live now, is barely 40 miles from the US Mexico border, so maybe this chamomile comes from the large Hispanic community that resides in North County? Chamomile is known as *manzanilla* in Mexico, and I have enjoyed a cup of manzanilla tea with more than my fair share of rolled tacos over the years. It turns out that I erroneously thought that everyone drank manzanilla tea at taco shops.

I spent the last year asking all my friends who grew up in North County with me if they remember the chamomile patches growing in dirt areas by the train tracks, the botanical gardens and the beach. No one remembers this. I also asked how many of them enjoy a cup of manzanilla tea with their burritos at the local taco shop only to find out that I am the only one.

Clearly, I must be wrong in my memory. But then a couple of years ago I had a meeting scheduled with the San Diego Botanic Garden Director, that was to take place in his office at the gardens. I was told to park in the employee parking lot, which turned out to be … wait for it … dirt! It was the sandy kind of dirt that I remembered from my youth. I was nicely dressed for my meeting complete with shoes but at this point I was wishing I were barefoot. The parking lot had a lovely view of the Pacific Ocean, complete with the salty sea air smell that I miss living in Vista. Nostalgia welled up in me and although Moonlight Beach itself couldn't be seen from this vantage point it was just a couple blocks away. As I walked through the lot toward the offices by the other cars, there it was! Chamomile growing in funny stunted patches. Of course, I immediately stepped on it (with my shoes on because I still had to get to my meeting) and there was that beguiling aroma I remembered of ocean breezes, spring sunshine and pineappley chamomile. I couldn't believe it. I almost cried because the combination was as unique and glorious as I remembered. Alas, still no one else remembers this, even though I keep asking, but that is okay.

I finally stopped asking my friends and resorted to the internet to find out about the chamomile of my youthful memories. And according to the California Native Plant Society's *Calscape*, California's top native plant website, there are two native "chamomiles": pineapple weed, *Matricaria discoidea,* and western pineapple weed, *Matricaria occidentalis.* Most likely of the two, *M. discoidea* is the plant I remember.

Matricaria discoidea, commonly known as pineapple weed, wild chamomile, and disc mayweed is an annual plant native to North America and Northeast Asia but which has become a cosmopolitan weed. It is in the family Asteraceae. The flowers exude a chamomile/pineapple aroma when crushed. They are edible and have been used in salads (although they may become bitter by the time the plant blooms) and to make herbal tea. Pineapple weed has been used for medicinal purposes, including for relief of gastrointestinal upset, infected sores, fevers, and postpartum anemia. The plant grows well in disturbed areas, especially those with poor, compacted soil. It can be seen blooming on footpaths, roadsides, and similar places in spring and early summer. In North America, it can be found from central Alaska down to California ... and into Baja California.

And now I know.

The next time you are in a taco shop, try having a cup of chamomile/ manzanilla tea with your flautas, it's delicious! Tell them Karen sent you.

Karen England lives, works and gardens on two steeply sloping acres in Vista, a small town in northern San Diego County, California, just nine miles as a crow flies from the Pacific Ocean. When she's not drinking herbal cocktails, she drinks tea. Find her on Instagram @edgehillherbfarm.

Need a Companion?

Diann Nance

If the pandemic taught us anything, it's how much we need relationships with other people. Plants may not be so different from us; they also develop relationships with other plants—and even with us. Because they entice us with their beauty, scent, and usefulness, we move them to new places. Humans long ago realized that some plants benefit from being planted close to other plants. Climbing beans planted among corn gives a trellis for the beans to climb on, and the beans provide some shade for the roots of the corn.

Chamomile was a constant in my mother's and in her mother's gardens. My grandmother believed chamomile could cure anything. I don't remember if she preferred one variety over the other; however, having come from German immigrants, my grandmother's *Alles zutraut,* meaning *can do anything*, probably referred to the German variety. I have assumed she meant as a benefit to people, but she may have been referring also to its benefits to other plants in the garden.

Many gardeners know that planting a variety of plants together can lead to a healthier garden than planting all the same variety. Researchers still have much to learn about how some plants benefit or suffer from proximity to other plants, but "there are five ways plants can affect one another: by improving the health and flavor of their neighbor, by interfering with the growth of their neighbor, by repelling pests, by trapping pests, or by attracting beneficial insects such as pest predators, parasites, and pollinators" (Kowalchik, 106).

Traditionally herbalists thought of chamomile as "the plant's physician," seeing its overall benefit to the health of a garden (82). It has been long believed that chamomile improves the growth and flavor of onions and cucumbers, but Darcy Larum adds cabbage, beans, broccoli, kale, brussels sprouts, cauliflower, kohlrabi, and even apples to that list. She goes on to suggest pairing chamomile with mint and basil to improve their scent.

The antifungal properties of chamomile make it a natural companion for plants susceptible to fungal problems or blight, such as zinnias, bee balm, phlox, tomatoes, and petunias (Larum, 1). Chamomile attracts beneficial insects, such as hoverflies and ladybugs, so plants susceptible to mites and aphids will benefit from a close relationship with chamomile (2).

Ken Druse includes a long list of herbs including chamomile that will grow in light shade, making it a good plant choice to shade the roots of clematis (Druse, 130).

There is much to learn about companion planting, and the research into this topic is ongoing. We can also learn much from our own experience and by experimenting in the garden. As you relax on your garden bench sipping a cup of chamomile tea with a friend, observe the plants benefiting from their companionship with one another.

References

Druse, Ken. "Want a Vegetable Garden too." *The New Shade Garden*. Stewart, Tabori, and Chang, New York, 2015.

Kowalchik, Claire and Hylton, William H., eds. *Rodale's Illustrated Encyclopedia of Herbs*. Rodale Press, Inc., 1987.

Larum, Darcy. "Chamomile Plant Companions: What to Plant with Chamomile." 15 February 2023. www. GardeningKnowHow.com. Accessed August 2024.

Diann Nance, born and raised on a farm in north central Texas, is presently living and growing herbs among the beautiful rolling hills of north central Tennessee. After a forty-year teaching career which included time spent in Texas, Taiwan, Germany, and finally Tennessee, she realized a long-held dream of starting a plant-growing business. As Diann's, she enjoyed eleven years of providing a wide variety of herbal plants for her community. Although Diann is now retired from the business of herbs, she still grows and uses herbs on a regular basis. Her interest in herbs and their uses in our daily lives can be attributed to her mother and grandmother who loved plants and shared their knowledge of herbs and plants in general.

Diann continues this tradition by growing plants, conducting presentations, and sharing the uses of herbs. She is a Master Gardener, a member of Beachaven Garden Club and the International Herb Association. She is a lifelong learner and may be contacted at dinance40@gmail.com.

Chamomile is a good choice for companion planting in a pollinator garden. *Susan Belsinger*

Author harvesting chamomile on her Wisconsin farm. *Susan Belsinger*

Calming Chamomile,
Matricaria chamomilla

Jane Hawley Stevens

Chamomile is one of those herbs that can do almost everything but wash your floor. In fact, I would use my leftover chamomile tea in my wash bucket for the floor, laundry, dishwasher, or shampoo due to its antiseptic and cleansing qualities.

Although diminutive, it is a powerhouse of activity. Chamomile is tiny but mighty.

Chamomile's action is calming and cooling. It seems so gentle, handling those soft, tiny white and yellow flowers, you would guess its actions would be mild and without much force. Wrong! It is as resolute as a dandelion seed pushing to bloom in a concrete walk.

Another magic trick, besides being the Princess of Panaceas, chamomile, although displaying white and yellow flowers, turns blue upon distillation. This is due to the azulene content in the essential oil, a dreamy, deep sky-blue color. This potent and pricey product is prized for its anti-inflammatory and antihistamine activities. According to Jim Duke, the late USDA herb researcher, educator, and author, azulene even has compounds that can stimulate liver regeneration. Duke continues listing chamomile qualities: antibacterial, antimycotic, ulcer protective, smooth muscle relaxant, along with the sedative effects.

There are two chamomiles with the same medicinal properties. *Matricaria chamomilla,* the common or German chamomile, and *Anthemis nobilis* (also known as *Chamaemelum nobilis*), the Roman chamomile. These two types of chamomile can be differentiated by this characteristic: the disk of *M. chamomilla* (wild) is hollow inside, while the disk of *A. nobilis* (Roman) is solid inside.

Once you get to know them you will notice from a distance the taller stature of the *M. chamomilla*, with a more expanded leaf structure. *Anthemis* is more compact, and stays closer to the ground when flowering, with noticeably soft, ferny foliage.

Matricaria grows better in my climate, in central Wisconsin, zone 4, with rich organic soil. We use a chamomile rake to harvest our flowers twice a week in the early summer. Rosettes and tap roots develop in late summer, get established, and bloom in the late spring when the previous year's rosettes push up the sunny yellow flowers. Once the heat of July arrives, the flowers, along with the foliage, fade into the Earth, setting up seeding our free crop of chamomile for next year!

Doctors throughout time, wherever chamomile grows on the globe, have relied on chamomile for stress and nervous tension from mild to severe cases. In South America chamomile is known as *manzanilla*, referring to the apple-like scent of the blossoms. In ancient Egypt, it was considered a sacred herb.

It would be hard to find an herb book that did not feature this delightful and potent healing plant, or an herbal doctor that would not have this dried flowerhead in their toolbox.

Chamomile is used in homeopathy. Often where there is inflammation causing tension with nervousness and irritability, the soothing quality of chamomile can resolve both problems.

As a budding herbalist, I used to wonder how one plant could have so many qualities, but when you consider the domino effect of how relaxing chamomile is on various body systems, it makes sense that it could assist with headaches, menstrual cramps, relaxing inflammation, spasms, and stomach pain. The bitter qualities of chamomile can assist in digestion and liver function. Dr. Jill Stansbury combines *Matricaria* with herbs to support cognitive function for those suffering from PTSD, yet Rudolf Weiss reminds us that "Much can be achieved by very simple means," adding "Chamomile is the most relaxing nervine herb in the Western world. It works on nerves and muscles, relaxing the whole body."

Chamomile is restorative and can be used as a base for tea to bring the stomach or nervous system back into balance.

It is easy to understand why chamomile is ruled by the Moon and the Sun.

Due to chamomile's soothing qualities, the ancient astrologers associated chamomile with the Moon. It was traditionally used to facilitate sweet dreams, reduce anxiety and depression, and encourage inner peace. The Moon rules the stomach, and chamomile is one of the best remedies for digestive discomfort, even releasing stored emotional tension from the past.

Chamomile could also be placed under the Sun, offered by Egyptians to the Sun god Ra. The Sun rules the heart, and the life-sustaining power of the Sun is surely captured in this potent plant. Herbs that relieve pain with their relaxing warmth are placed under this rulership.

I have used chamomile throughout the decades of raising my children, calming them when they stayed home sick. Seeking the sleep-inducing and antimicrobial qualities, I watched them rest comfortably and get well quickly with the chamomile and honey-filled teapot nearby. The only negative effect was that my daughter, Savanna, has told me she doesn't enjoy chamomile tea anymore because it reminds her of the few times that she was sick growing up.

This herb is a great choice to calm a fussy child; chamomile is a great baby medicine. Matthew Wood, midwestern herbalist, author, and teacher reported that fussy babies demanding to be held and not being comforted when picked up (or fussing for a toy, only to throw it when it is received) can be calmed with a simple infusion.

Chamomile Bath or Footbath

Chamomile is so soothing to the psyche and body. This chamomile bath could be used to calm a restless adult or child.

Makes enough for 1 bath

1/4 ounce dried, or 1/2 ounce fresh, *Lavandula angustifolia*, lavender flowers/
1/4 ounce dried, or 1/2 ounce fresh, *Matricaria chamomilla*, chamomile flowers
1/4 ounce dried, or 1/2 ounce, fresh, *Rosa* spp., rose petals

Combine the flowers and cover with water in a stockpot; briefly simmer, just for a minute or so. Let steep, covered, for 15 minutes.

Pour into a bath or container for a foot bath to calm and reset the nervous system.

Jane Hawley Stevens plants, harvests, and creates herbal wellness for her brand, Four Elements Organic Herbals, from her 130-acre farm in Wisconsin. She and her husband, David, received the Organic Farmer of the Year award in 2020. Jane is a pioneer in organic farming and natural products communities and has been certified organic since 1989, specializing in herbs since graduating with a horticulture degree in the 80s.

Jane believes in cultivating Nature's wisdom with its beauty and rhythms, knowing it is up to all of us to contribute to our planet's health and sustainability.

She spends her time gardening, hiking, biking, or skiing to be surrounded by the beauty and awe that can only be experienced outdoors. You can find her at night, gazing at the stars and planets with reverence for the opportunity to be an advocate for Nature and all of its wonderment.

Dewy chamomile at Four Elements Organic Herbals farm, Wisconsin.
Susan Belsinger

Emilia in her garden from Teseida. Boccacio *www.wikipedia.org*

Tudor style chamomile bench. Morehavens Chamomile Nursery.
https://www.camomilelawns.co.uk

A Very Tudor Camomile

Skye Suter

A Tudor styled court garden was meant for recreation, meditation and enjoyment. These gardens were planted with beauty, scent and enjoyment in mind. During the Tudor period camomile was held in high regard for its fragrance. It was one of many plants the Tudors planted as a ground cover that was meant to be walked upon, as the scents would be released as a sort of aromatherapy.

There are two ways to spell the name of this plant—"chamomile" the American way, and "camomile" the British way. The two are interchangeable and are used in both countries, but camomile is the more traditional English spelling and likely closer to the way it was spelled during Tudor times.

Camomile's long history of use proclaims it as a perfect all-around herb. Documentation of camomile has been found in ancient Egyptian hieroglyphics, where it was referred to as "the flower of the sun." There are many references to camomile from ancient Roman and Greek notables of the times, such as Pliny and Dioscorides.

Extracted oils from camomiles have been used as a soothing herb in aromatherapy. *Matricaria chamomilla*, also known as *M. recutita*, or German camomile, is referred to as "mother's best friend," and is preferred for teas and tinctures. It is used to calm stomachs, wash wounds and soothe skin irritations as well as for rheumatic pain and hemorrhoids. In medieval times it was popular as a strewing herb and was used to ward off evil spirits. *Anthemis tinctoria,* also known as Dyer's Camomile, was used to color wools, silks and cottons. In culinary applications camomile is used to add an apple-like flavor to jams, liquors, candies, and ice cream. *Chamaemelum nobile,* English or Roman camomile, is used for teas as well, but is better outside as a bedding plant or ground cover.

The Renaissance started in Italy and spanned across Europe, spreading enlightened ideas and prosperous times. The Tudor era refers strictly to England and the dynastic house of the Plantagenets. The Renaissance and Tudor periods came at the end of the medieval period.

The House of Tudor ruled from 1485 to 1603 and died out with Queen Elizabeth I, who had no children. The term "Elizabethan Era" refers to the time of Elizabeth's reign and is also considered part of the Tudor era. During this time camomile became closely associated with the House of Tudor and was especially popular in gardens for its aroma and to walk or sit upon.

During and around the Tudor period there is an abundance of camomile documentation in herbals as well as in literary works. In Anthony Askham's *A Little Herball* from 1550, he wrote: "This herbe is called camomyl … if it be doike with wine it will beke the stone and distroyeth the yellow evel. It helpeth with akying and the diseas of lyver …" Elizabethan herbalist Gerard called camomile "a remedy against all wearisomenesse."

The Elizabethans and Tudors enjoyed the sweet smell of camomile, and in 1574, the poet Spencer wrote about his experience of walking on a chamomile lawn in "Breathful Camomile." In *A New Orchard and Garden* (1648) William Lawson wrote, "Large walks, broad and long, close and open, like the Tempe groves in Thessaly, raised with gravel and sand, having seats and banks of Camomile; all this delights the mind, and brings health to the body." In addition to camomile, the poet Thomas Philipps mentioned many flowers popular at the time including columbine, daisies, gillyflowers, barge, savory, lavender, primroses and violets.

And we can't forget the Bard. Shakespeare refers to camomile in *King Henry IV, Part I* (2.4): "For though the camomile, the more it is trodden on the faster it grows, yet youth, the more it is wasted the sooner it wears." A more modern-day literary connection is a novel entitled *The Camomile Lawn*. It is the best-known book by author Mary Wesley, an English novelist who worked in MI5 during World War II.

A Tudor garden was highly regarded as a place for meditation, recreation and exercise, while the larger surrounding cultivated areas were important for supplying fruit, vegetables, herbs and flowers for food, medicine and other useful products.

Tudor gardens incorporated several interesting features that often included the use of camomile. Some of these elements included "mounds" or "mounts," scented pathways, arbors and turf seats. Mounts were man-made hills, constructed to offer sweeping views of the formal gardens, as well as the surrounding landscape.

The idea of a mount is reminiscent of Motte and Bailey castle construction, which consisted of a fortification or structure on top of a hill, with a commanding view of farms and the landscape beyond. Mounts often had winding pathways or steps leading to the top of the mound, which was topped by a sitting area, an arbor, or a summer house. Sweet smelling flowers such as camomile often bordered these pathways, so visitors would release beautiful aromas as they walked on the camomile and brushed by the flowers lining the pathways.

Turf seats were built freestanding, or sometimes against a wall or around a tree. They could be situated either on a mount or other area of a Tudor garden. Turf seats sometimes had an arbor constructed over or around them. The arms of a turf seat were made from brick or stone. Faced with stone or brick as well, a turf seat was basically a solid earth construction bench with the seat planted in camomile, pennyroyal or grass. The rest of a Tudor garden would be laid out symmetrically with pathways through knot gardens or other formally laid out garden beds. These pathways were also planted with camomile.

In medieval Europe and England, camomile was cultivated alongside other herbs, flowers and vegetables. Camomile is an excellent companion plant; it is sometimes called the "plant doctor." It repels pests and enhances the growth and well-being of neighboring plants.

While the Tudors enjoyed the sweet smell of chamomile, they also appreciated the scent and visual beauty of many other plants. Some plants commonly cultivated in Tudor gardens included hyssop, purple iris, holly-hock, columbine, wallflower, English lavender, daffodil, primrose, roses (*Rosa gallica*, *Rosa alba*, sweet briar rose), sweet violet, white lupin, yellow lupin, rose campion, sweet rocket, honesty, pot marigold, Christmas rose, peony, poppy, saffron crocus, carnations (pinks), foxgloves, borage, English bluebells and many more. Some plants that were newly introduced to England during the reign of Henry VIII and his children included snowdrops, snapdragon, red-flowered daisy, plumed cockscomb, cornflower, curry plant, spike lavender, French lavender, cotton lavender, Jacob's ladder, Turk's cap lily, African marigold, nasturtium, rock rose, cyclamen, Spanish dagger, cornelian cherry, and apricot.

Artist's rendition of the 14th century Whittington Castle mount garden.
www.thegardenhistory.blog

Tudor gardens were influenced by earlier medieval gardens and by contemporary styles on the continent, namely Italian Renaissance and French formal gardens. Visual and written records of Tudor gardens are somewhat sparse, so some of what we see today are recreated based upon the perceptions and sensibilities of the Victorians and the early 20th century.

There are many examples of these gardens throughout England, but the most famous camomile lawns can be found at Buckingham Palace where they are part of the palace's 39-acre garden. The lawns are in several garden areas including the Main Lawn, the Rose Garden and near the Herbaceous Border. In 1703 the Duke of Buckingham arranged for a more formal layout. The most famous camomile lawn was originally planted for George III. In the 1820's George IV commissioned William Townsend Aiton, head gardener at Kew, to remodel the gardens completely. It was Aiton who created the lake and the broad stretches of lawn famous for its camomile.

Taller, upright varieties of camomile are grown for teas, medicines, and bedding plants, while the low-growing cultivars are appropriate for ground covers or turf seats. Camomile is very different from grass ground cover, as it has an amazing sweet and fruity apple-like scent, which is released by walking over it. This scent is especially strong after a rain.

Camomile lawns in the past had one disadvantage—they needed to be trimmed. In the 1930s, Dorothy Sewart planted a camomile cutting in the garden of her 18th century stone cottage in Cornwall. This camomile spread to form a low-growing plant which never flowered, and formed a fragrant, rich green lawn which did not turn brown in dry weather. She had been extremely fortunate in producing the cultivar that came to be called 'Treneague'.

The two best varieties of camomile use for creating today's ground covers are *Chamaemelum nobile* 'Treneague' and dwarf camomile, *Chamaemelum nobile*. 'Treneague' never flowers but has a wonderfully sweet fragrance. Since there are no flowers, there is no pollen, which is good for hay fever sufferers.

Dwarf camomile sometimes has a few single, daisy-like flowers in late summer. It is grows slightly taller than 'Treneague' and the stems are a little longer and thicker. Both are ideal for growing around plants, such as roses, and around water features, on graves, or for edging paths.

A successful camomile lawn or walkway requires correct cultivation and conditions. An open, sunny site is best for a camomile lawn, but it will do well in dappled light. Too much shade causes patchy cover. These perennial plants require six or more hours of sun and can be grown in USDA zones 4 to 9. They prefer light sandy loam and will not do well in very dry, stony conditions or heavy clay. Watering may be required during an excessively dry spell.

Camomile is toxic to pets if ingested, so should not be grown in areas that pets frequent. Allergic reactions may cause vomiting, diarrhea, or bleeding.

Charles Marshall, in his *Introduction to the Knowledge and Practice of Gardening* (1805), gives directions for making camomile "green or carpet walks" by planting the sets about 9 or 10 inches apart. Walking on the plants, or rolling over them, naturally spreads the runners.

To start a new lawn or path, the area should first be prepared by thoroughly removing all the weeds. After clearing the area you might want to let it sit for a couple of weeks to allow any dormant weed seeds to show themselves. Small rooted runners or potted plants that can be divided are best. For planting a lawn, space plants 4 to 8 inches apart depending on their size. They are best planted in mid to late spring when they are actively growing and have time to establish before winter. Water well until established. New lawns should not be walked on for at least 12 weeks and traffic should be kept to a minimum for up to a year. This camomile does not survive wet or cold winters very well, so it is probably best to cultivate camomile ground cover in limited areas, or include additional plants like thyme, pennyroyal or grass in the planting.

Nearly all 17th century garden books give directions for the treatment of camomile lawns. Under "October" in John Evelyn's *Kalenarium Hortense*, we find: "it will now be good to Beat Roll and Mow carpet walks and camomile for now the ground is supple and it will even all inequalities."

Today there is no need to mow if using the non-flowering dwarf cultivar 'Treneague'. If the growth looks a bit scraggly in late summer, just trim it lightly. Since 'Treneague' is a non-flowering cultivar, it will not come true from seed and needs to be propagated by division.

Cultivars of Roman or English *Chamaemelum nobile* are perennials and good for ground covers, while German camomile, *Matricaria recutita*, an annual, is better for teas and other uses. The species, *C. nobile,* and its flowering cultivars, are just as aromatic but not ideal for walking on as they grow too tall. The flowers will need to be diligently trimmed off or dead patches will appear. *C. nobile* 'Flore Pleno' is low growing, reaching a height of only six inches. However, it also needs regular deadheading to prevent bare patches. Therefore, the non-flowering cultivar 'Treneague' is a much better, lower maintenance option.

Maintenance of a camomile lawn requires occasional replanting, as dead patches might appear when individual plants age and the centers die out. Very cold or wet winters might also cause patches of die-out. It is best to replant in areas when the plants die out to maintain a thick carpet of growth and repel weeds. The camomile lawns grown at Buckingham Palace and other places are combined with grass, so that there will be more even growth.

If you want to add some of the romanticism of Tudor camomile to your own garden, add a camomile pathway or construct a turf seat. Otherwise, enjoy this versatile herb in one of its many other soothing ways.

References

"Chamomile lawns." https://www.rhs.org.uk/lawns/chamomile-lawns. Accessed August 6, 2024.

"Genteel Chamomile." https://www.homestead.org/herbs/genteel-chamomile/. Accessed June 3, 2024.

"How do I grow Chamomile, and can it be used as a lawn?" NYBG LuEsther T. Mertz Library Plant & Research Help, https://libanswers.nybg.org/faq/223001. Accessed July 17, 2024.

Morehavens Chamomile Nursery. https://www.camomilelawns.co.uk/pages/history#:~:text=The%20most%20famous%20chamomile%20lawns,to%20make%20sure%20it%20thrives. Accessed July 6, 2024.

"Mounts and Mounds 1: reusing the past." https://thegardenstrust.blog/2015/09/12/mounts-and-mounds/. Accessed July 17, 2024.

St. Clare Garden. https://www.scu.edu/stclaregarden/stclare/medievalgardens/#:~:text=The%20garden%20features%20other%20elements,)%2C%20a%20gravel%20walk%20way%2C. Accessed July 17, 2024.

"The Early Tudor Garden." https://tudorsdynasty.com/the-early-tudor-garden-circa-1490-1550/. Accessed July 17, 2024.

Rohde, Eleanor Sinclair. *The Story of the Garden.* https://books.google.com/books?id=UWhNDwAAQBAJ&l pg=PT167&dq=The%20famous%20camomile%20lawn%20at%20 buckingham%20palace%20side&pg=PT165#v=onepage&q=The%20 famous%20camomile%20lawn%20at%20buckingham%20palace%20 side&f=false. Accessed July 6, 2024.

Various articles. *Science Direct.* https://www.sciencedirect.com/ topics/agricultural-and-biological-sciences/chamomile#:~:text=In%20 the%20middle%20ages%2C%20chamomile,belongs%20to%20the%20 Asteraceae%20family. Accessed June 3, 2024.

"Why is Camomile Suddenly Everywhere?" *The New York Times Style Magazine.* https://www.nytimes.com/2022/10/14/t-magazine/chamomile-food-fashion.html. Accessed July 16, 2024.

Skye Suter has been involved with art and plants for most of her life. She worked at a newspaper as an Art Director and wrote garden and food columns. Skye worked at a botanical garden and for other non-profits in marketing and producing graphic design, as well as educational programming.

She is a member of the International Herb Association, where she was formerly on the board, and is a member of the Herb Society of America. Locally, she is a member of PPSEAWA New York and the Staten Island Herb Society, as well as a past president. She is on the Board of Friends of Blue Heron Park, Inc. where she enjoys walking the trails and guiding plant-related programming.

Currently she is a freelance writer, occasional illustrator and graphic designer. Her disciplines are showcased through organizations that reflect her interests in plants, nature, art, crafting, cooking and especially herbs.

Skye can be reached at skyesuter@gmail.com.

Deadheading German Chamomile

Chuck Voigt

When I was starting my field research with herbs at the Vegetable Research Farm, south of the University of Illinois campus in Champaign, Illinois, I did a variety of things, including a raised bed experiment, using ten common herbs in raised beds, with various soil amendments. I also collected a wide variety of herb seeds and plants to grow and evaluate in an observation trial. As it turns out, German Chamomile, *Matricaria chamomilla,* was among these.

Also at this time, I acquired my first student employee, a work study horticulture student, let's call him "Jim" (not his real name, but he's in his 50s now, and may have a very different life). Jim was known around the department as something of an underachiever, very bright, but not always highly motivated in the classroom. I think he enjoyed working with me on my little half-acre herb patch, though, and he never complained, no matter how dirty and menial the work was that we were doing. Later, I had a young woman who worked with me, who compared what we did to "Little House on the Prairie," which is where she imagined herself as we were grubbing potatoes or some other crop out of the soil,

Back to Jim, he and I were cleaning up some "volunteer" herbs, which had self-sown between the rows of the current year's plantings. Among these was a fairly healthy contingent of German Chamomile plants, brightly flowering and exuding their characteristic fragrance. Jim was enchanted by this scent, which was new to him, so he filled a couple of paper grocery bags with the plants we had pulled from among this year's evaluations, intent on trying out the tea. Unlike when I was an undergraduate, Jim had a car, and always drove himself to where we were working. He tossed the bags of chamomile into the trunk at the end of the day and was off.

As I had learned in the hours we spent sweating in the herb garden together, Jim had an affinity for one special rock band, the Grateful Dead, whose devotees are lovingly known as "Dead Heads." This may go a long way toward explaining Jim's lack of focus in the classroom, and his status as a known underachiever. At any rate, he and his fellow Dead Heads packed up and hit the road to attend a scheduled concert—I forget if it was in Columbus, Ohio, or even farther away to the east. As they were driving through the night, they all found themselves drifting off to sleep, as the fruity aroma of the chamomile permeated the interior of the car, from where it resided in the trunk. They were finally forced to pull over and dump the bags on the side of the road, to avoid causing a collision when they all fell asleep.

I had told Jim that chamomile was very soothing, and made a good bedtime beverage, but he never imagined it would become a sedative for the whole carload of Dead Heads. He was convinced of the power of herbs at that point and vowed never again to mix the Grateful Dead and German Chamomile. I hope he never doubted what I said about herbs again, and that's the story of Deadheading German Chamomile.

Charles Voigt is a retired faculty member at the University of Illinois at Urbana-Champaign. He was a state vegetable and herb specialist there from 1988 through 2015. In 1989, he was on the steering committee that wrote the bylaws forming the Illinois Herb Association. He first presented a talk at the International Herb Growers and Marketers Association (later renamed International Herb Association or IHA) in 1991. He was head of the host committee for IHA's 1995 conference in Chicago, IL, and again in 2010 for the conference in Collinsville, IL. At the Portland, OR, IHA conference in 2001 he received IHA's Service award, and in 2010, in Collinsville, IL, their Professional Award. In 2014 in Toronto, he presented the Otto Richter Memorial Lecture at the annual IHA conference. He served on the IHA Program Committee for many years and has been the chair of the Horticulture Committee since 1997. This committee has been instrumental in choosing and promoting Herbs of the Year. Chuck is currently the chair of the IHA Foundation, as well. He also wrote the popular book, *Vegetable Gardening in the Midwest*, with his vegetable mentor, Dr. Joseph Vandemark. One of Chuck's goals in retirement is to sing in 100 gardens.

German chamomile blooms and clouds. *Susan Belsinger*

German chamomile, *Matricaria recutita* is a reseeding annual; once established it will reappear in the garden in early spring.
www.commons.wikimedia.org

Matricaria, One of Many Herbal Harbingers of Spring

Tina Marie Wilcox

German Chamomile (*Matricaria recutita*) is an herb for tea that grows reliably in the Kitchen Garden at the Ozark Folk Center State Park in Mountain View, Arkansas. It is a perpetual, self-sowing annual that germinates in late February and early March with chervil (*Anthriscus cerefolium*), chickweed (*Stellaria media*), corn salad (*Valerianella radiata*), deadnettle (*Lamium purpureum*), henbit (*Lamium amplexicaule*), Johnny-jump-ups (*Viola tricolor*), and shepherd's purse (*Capsella bursa-pastoris)*. All these herbs grow together, rampantly, filling the once cold, barren garden with verdant green, the fragrance of fresh chlorophyll and essential oils, and splash the garden with colorful pigments that refresh the senses and bring on spring fever and a feeding frenzy for all life warming up after winter.

Each species, in its own time and habit, multiplies cells to produce stems and leaves, most edible, that support flowers for pollinators, herbalists and edible flower aficionados. They then set seed throughout May and June. By July, the cool season annuals have distributed seeds for the next season and are already decomposing to feed the soil biome. These herbs live useful lives, providing food and medicine for knowledgeable human beings, nectar for insects, browse for wildlife (and the wild at heart), and biomass for decomposers to regenerate the soil.

Unlike most of the spring volunteers mentioned, chamomile did not find its way to the Kitchen Garden on its own. The chamomile in the Kitchen Garden was introduced a couple of decades ago because of an organic gardening experiment in the park's greenhouse.

A flat of seedlings was infected by a damping off disease caused by a pathogenic fungus that was encouraged by improper watering. I decided to try watering the surviving seedlings with chamomile sun tea because I had the flowers in bulk and had read or heard that chamomile helps other plants.

In the end, every one of the original seedlings died and, wait for it, were replaced by a full flat of chamomile plants! Being an opportunistic sort, I planted the chamomile in the Kitchen Garden where it has taken up residence. In hindsight, had I bagged and disposed of the infected flat immediately, as would have been the prudent thing to do with fungal infected plants in the greenhouse, I would not have enjoyed the presence of German chamomile all these years.

This herb gardener revels in intimate knowledge of the plants in her garden. Herb gardening is science and art, with processes that build soil, observational skills, and the proliferation of life while one is planting, irrigating, and harvesting. The word *weeds* and the phrase *just weeding* do not apply.

In March, the Kitchen Garden pathways must first be cleared because non-gardeners will be coming out from the kitchen to cut rosemary, thyme, oregano, and sage and must be able to see how to get around in the garden without walking on the garden beds. A compost/chicken run basket is filled with most of the volunteer spring ephemerals from the walkways. The chickens love the fresh greens and the insects that cling to the leaves and flowers. The spring compost pile, that starts with carbon from the previous autumn's deciduous tree leaves, needs the nitrogen from the green leaves to maintain the carbon to nitrogen (C:N) balance of 30:1 for efficient decay. The pathways provide plenty for both the chickens and the compost.

The foraging basket gets salad and potherb ingredients that are growing too close to the perennial culinary herbs. These include the chickweed, corn salad, dead nettle, henbit, Johnny-jump-ups, and young shepherd's purse. The tender tops of these plants are snipped into the forage basket and shaded with a tea towel. The rest goes to the compost/chicken run basket.

Delicate chervil is best snipped directly into a jar and covered with white wine vinegar. I do this every couple of years for personal use. It is important that the chervil go to seed so that this harbinger of spring continues in case a chef wants us to have it for one of our special herb dinners.

The chamomile plants are often carefully transplanted from the pathways and from around the perennial herbs to empty spaces in the garden. Thinning plants that are closer than eight inches apart is important for flower production. The little daisy-like display comes later in the spring so this is the time to create a mass planting within the Kitchen Garden. You too can identify the fine, feathery, fragrant foliage of young chamomile volunteers and set them where you want them to grow and perpetuate.

In late May through June, very early in the morning, this gardener brings a small harvest basket to the garden, along with a trash bag and the big harvest basket. By this time in the growing season, the spring ephemerals have set seed. The garden's appearance needs brightening by harvesting faded annual herbs. Planting, pruning, and harvesting is too much fun to call these activities work. The only real work in the Kitchen Garden is ferreting out nutsedge (*Cyperus esculentus*) rhizomes and nutlets and stuffing them into the trash bag bound for the landfill. This is work because one can never win, no matter how determined.

After the sun has dried the dew, and the grit from the nutsedge battle is rinsed from the hands and face, it is time to sit and watch the bees and butterflies flitting amongst the chamomile and occasionally pinch perfect flowers into the small basket. This mild harvest calms the spirit and provides reward for the never-ending war on nutsedge.

I have sipped warm chamomile infusions during times of stress and poured it through my hair as a final rinse to see if I could notice more blonde highlights. I found the sensations of warmth and the distinctive aroma pleasing and can report that my sun-bleached hair had streaks of blond anyway and did not respond to the short-term experiment.

I have a friend, Angelia, who, like me, keeps chickens. We were recently discussing how to encourage our hens to be happy while protecting them from predators. (Everyone loves chicken, including birds of prey, racoons, possums, skunks, dogs, bobcats, and ferrets.) Keeping the flock cooped up and in runs keeps them safe from predators most of the time, however, we both think that our chickens get peckish because they cannot live a free-range lifestyle. Angelia shared that she makes chamomile tea for her hens and observes that they seem more content after drinking the infusion. I believe the yellow center in the flowers would make my hen's yolks an even richer orange in color with the addition of chamomile flowers in their diet.

I have left it to other authors to describe the chemical constituents and benefits of chamomile flowers and their essential oils. Instead, I hope I have described the ease of growing and using this charming and practical herb and inspired fellow gardeners to introduce it to their gardens.

Tina Marie Wilcox has been the head gardener and herbalist at the Ozark Folk Center's Heritage Herb Garden in Mountain View, Arkansas, since 1984. She tends the gardens, plans and coordinates annual herbal events and facilitates the production of sale plants, seeds, and herbal products for the park. She is a well-seasoned herbal educator, entertainer and, with Susan Belsinger, co-authored *the creative herbal home*.

Tina currently serves as president of the International Herb Association. She is a member of the Herb Society of America-Ozark Unit and was awarded the Nancy Putnam Excellence in Horticulture Award in 2017 by the Herb Society of America. In 2023, Tina collaborated with other herbalists, foragers, and gardeners to create teaching gardens on the Capitol Mall in Washington D.C. for the Smithsonian Folklife Festival which celebrated the Ozarks.

Tina's philosophy is based upon experiencing the joy of the process, perpetrating no harm, and understanding life through play with plants and people.

Chamomile seedlings ready to plant out. *Susan Belsinger*

Chamomile growing alongside clover and mint in the Heritage Herb Garden at the Ozark Folk Center State Park. *Susan Belsinger*

Stress-relief tea
Holy basil and chamomile
Sleep like a baby

Susan Belsinger

Chamomile in the Kitchen

Buttermilk pie is subtly flavored with dried chamomile flowers—both in the filling and the crust. *Susan Belsinger*

Buttermilk Pie with Chamomile in a Pecan Crust

Susan Belsinger

This delicious recipe is adapted from The Beekman 1802 Heirloom Dessert Cookbook *by Josh Kilmer-Purcell, Brent Ridge and Sandy Gluck. I tweaked it a bit and had an inspiration to infuse chamomile in the buttermilk overnight, which gives a mild, lovely, unusual flavor along with just a hint of fresh ginger.*

I enjoy this pie barely warm or at room temperature. If there are leftovers, refrigerate, and remove to stand at room temperature about 30 minutes before serving. It is delightful as is, although I like a few toasted pecan halves for garnish. It could be served with fresh sliced peaches or nectarines, berries or lightly poached pears. It is very rich, so a little goes a long way.

Makes a 10-inch pie; serves 8 to 12

Buttermilk infusion

1 1/2 cup buttermilk
2 tablespoons dried chamomile flowers
1 scant tablespoon finely grated fresh gingerroot

Combine the buttermilk, chamomile and grated ginger in a jar with a tight-fitting lid and shake well. Refrigerate overnight or for at least a few hours. When ready to make the filling, pour the buttermilk through a strainer, pressing on the herbs to remove the essence.

Crust

1 1/4 cups unbleached flour
1/2 cup pecans
1 tablespoon organic sugar
Scant 1/2 teaspoon sea salt
1 tablespoon dried chamomile flowers
5 tablespoons unsalted butter, chilled and cut into pieces
1 extra large egg

Combine the flour, pecans, sugar, salt and chamomile in the bowl of a food processor and pulse until the nuts are finely ground. Add the butter and egg and pulse until the dough just starts to come together—don't let it form into a ball. Turn the dough out and gather it together; if it seems dry add a teaspoon or two of water. Pat it into a disk, wrap in plastic wrap and refrigerate for a minimum of 30 minutes or overnight.

Flour your work surface and roll the dough out with a floured rolling pin into about a 12- to 13-inch round. Carefully transfer the dough to a 10-inch pie plate and press the dough against the bottom and sides of the pan, making sure that it is evenly thin. Or alternatively, flatten the disk of dough in the plastic wrap and then turn it out into the pie plate and use your fingers to gently spread/push the dough out evenly to cover the bottom, sides and rim of the pie plate. If you rolled the dough, use a knife to trim the dough leaving a little overhang over the rim. Fold this over, doubling the dough around the edge. Crimp the edge of the crust onto the rim with a fork or your fingers. Chill the pie crust for at least an hour.

When ready to bake the crust, preheat the oven to 400°F. Cover the pie dough with parchment paper leaving an overhang to cover the edges and add pie weights or dried beans to cover the bottom. Bake the crust for 15 minutes. Remove the parchment with the weights and bake for 10 minutes more until lightly browned. Remove to cool on a baking rack and reduce oven temp to 325°F.

Filling

1 cup organic sugar
3 tablespoons + 1 teaspoon cornstarch
Large pinch salt
1 1/2 cups infused buttermilk
6 tablespoons unsalted butter, melted
4 extra-large eggs

Combine the sugar, cornstarch and salt in the bowl of a food processor and pulse to mix. Add the buttermilk, melted butter and eggs; pulse to combine. Pour the filling into the warm pie shell. Bake for about 50 minutes until the filling is set and just barely wobbly in the center. Remove the pie to a baking rack to cool before serving. Cut into slices. If desired, garnish with toasted pecans casually scattered over each slice once plated (about 1 scant cup for the whole pie).

For a lovely tisane, strain flowers from chamomile infusion after it has steeped for about 5 minutes. *Susan Belsinger*

Chamomile Tea and Me ~ Tisanes, Syrups and Cocktails

Gert Coleman

For many years, I would only drink black tea (*Camellia sinensis*)—the darker the better. With its slowly released caffeine, ability to increase focus, and literary connection to British drawing rooms, *Camellia sinesis* is still my go-to beverage. Iced or hot, with or without sugar and lemon, I particularly love the robust Assam variety imbibed by the working class in all my beloved murder mysteries.

Herbally though, my favorite beverage these days is the gentle and powerful chamomile. Variously spelled Camomile or Chamomile, it should be a staple in your tea cupboard and herb garden. Chamomile's daisy-like flower—a golden center with a ray of white petals—adds charm to garden borders with its pretty and diminutive stature. When gently stepped on in lawns and paths, Roman chamomile (*Chamaemelum nobile*) springs back readily and aromatically—truly a "friend in low places." Bright green in the spring before many other herbs, this plant remains green and cheerful long after yarrow and other herbs have faded to autumnal grays and browns.

Chamomile flowers dry without much effort and make a wonderful base for many healthful beverages. In the Language of Flowers, chamomile symbolizes resilience in adversity, help against weariness, initiative, patience, and ingenuity. Quite impressive for a lowly plant!

As an herbalist, I relish drinking herbal infusions or what Agatha Christie's super sleuth Hercule Poirot calls *tisanes*. While they lack the jolt of caffeine, herbal tisanes contain minerals and nutrients that support good health. I like many herbal teas but reliably come back to chamomile. For one thing, chamomile can be readily found, either fresh or prepackaged, at farmer's markets or supermarkets. It's typically one of the two herbal teas offered at restaurants, hotels, or friend's homes (the other being peppermint). And, like black tea, chamomile tea tastes good hot or iced, alone or in combinations with other herbs and spices.

Long known for its tonic qualities—as an antidote to anxiety, restlessness, and insomnia, relief for tight, tense muscles, digestive woes, and intermittent fevers—chamomile has long been found in the home apothecary. Thomas Jefferson listed chamomile as one of the herbs to be grown in the Monticello kitchen garden and it was always found in medieval and Renaissance gardens for its soothing scent, healing properties, and household uses. Even today, chamomile grows in the Aromatherapy Border in London's Chelsea Garden for its role in medicines and perfumes.

Chamomile offers literary appeal to inveterate readers and tea drinkers as well. Chamomile was well known in the Elizabethan era. In Shakespeare's historical drama *Henry IV* (c. 1596), Falstaff uses chamomile, to suggest to Prince Hal, or Harry, the future king, that both humility and strength come from *surviving* crises of all kinds:

> *Harry, I do not only marvel where thou spendest thy time, but also how thou art accompanied: for though the camomile, the more it is trodden on the faster it grows, yet youth, the more it is wasted the sooner it wears.* I *Henry IV*, II, iv, 441.

In the following poem by British poet Katherine Mansefield (1888-1923), chamomile's familiar image as a restful cup of tea supports a sense of calm, ease, and intimacy. Inside a warm, cozy cottage, a couple relaxes with chamomile tea while outside the sea roars and the wind tumbles blossoms to the ground. Perhaps a spot of romance is in the air?

Camomile Tea

Outside the sky is light with stars;
There's a hollow roaring from the sea.
And, alas! for the little almond flowers,
The wind is shaking the almond tree.

How little I thought, a year ago,
In the horrible cottage upon the Lee
That he and I should be sitting so
And sipping a cup of camomile tea.

Light as feathers the witches fly,
The horn of the moon is plain to see;
By a firefly under a jonquil flower
A goblin toasts a bumble-bee.

We might be fifty, we might be five,
So snug, so compact, so wise are we!
Under the kitchen-table leg
My knee is pressing against his knee.

Our shutters are shut, the fire is low,
The tap is dripping peacefully;
The saucepan shadows on the wall
Are black and round and plain to see.

In Germany, chamomile is known as a*lles zutraut,* or "capable of anything." Thus we see in poetry and in real life that chamomile is a panacea for many things, whether we are fifty or five.

Or as herbalist Matthew Wood suggests, chamomile is good for "babies of any age" (*Earthwise* 178). In Beatrix Potter's beloved children's book, *The Tale of Peter Rabbit* (1902), little Peter sneaks into Mr. McGregor's garden, despite being warned not to by his mother. He eats so many vegetables that he feels sick. But his troubles have just begun when an angry Mr. McGregor discovers him and the damage he has caused to the garden. Peter runs for his life, dodging garden pots, slipping under fences, and dropping his blue coat with yellow buttons in the process:

Peter never stopped running or looked behind him till he got home to the big fir-tree. He was so tired that he flopped down upon the nice soft sand on the floor of the rabbit-hole, and shut his eyes. His mother was busy cooking; she wondered what he had done with his clothes. It was the second little jacket and pair of shoes that Peter had lost in a fortnight!

I am sorry to say that Peter was not very well during the evening. His mother put him to bed, and made some camomile tea; and she gave a dose of it to Peter! 'One table-spoonful to be taken at bed-time.' But Flopsy, Mopsy, and Cotton-tail had bread and milk and blackberries, for supper.

Peter jumped out of the window, upsetting three plants. Beatrix Potter
www.projectgutenberg.org

Chamomile Teas, Tisanes, and Infusions

While I often drink chamomile straight, chamomile can also be combined with other herbs to create infusions or tisanes. While the term *tisane* typically refers to non-caffeinated herbal teas, the terms *tisane*, *tea*, and *infusion* are used interchangeably here. Sip a cup of herbal tea for pleasure or as a simple homemade remedy. Herbal teas can be drunk warm or cold, and kept for a day or so on the counter, or up to 5 days in the refrigerator.

I love teapots and brewing a proper cup of tea with a tea basket strainer and a tea cozy to keep it warm is a daily ritual. But if you don't have these accessories, making tea is simple: pour boiling, or nearly boiled water, over tea leaves, herbal or otherwise, whether in a teapot or mug or glass jar, and let them sit for several minutes. This is called *steeping* or *brewing*. Then use a small strainer to hold back the leaves as you pour the tea into your favorite mug. Or, for convenience, purchase a box of chamomile teabags and use accordingly. Note: To cover or not to cover? Many herbalists cover the brew while steeping to keep the flavor and nutrients inside. It's an arguable point. When I brew a cup of chamomile with a teabag, I leave it uncovered, but when I brew a pot of chamomile tea, I cover it with a tea cozy.

Chamomile's apple-like fragrance and flavor is sweetest after five minutes of steeping. Longer than that, its medicinal bitter qualities come to the forefront, and if you're new to drinking chamomile tea, it's best to see how you like the flavor first. For a more medicinal dose, steep for 10 minutes or more, but be aware that the taste will become somewhat bitter, which is actually desirable for soothing the digestive tract.

Made too much chamomile tea? No problem. Leftover chamomile tea has many uses. In the kitchen, you can use it to clean cutting boards, wash out refrigerators, and mop up sticky countertops. Herbal expert Nancy Arrowsmith recommends dipping strong-smelling pieces of fish, game, or meat in chamomile tea to remove offensive odors (*Essential Herbal Wisdom* 337). In the apothecary, you can use it as a wash to soothe sunburned skin, itchy bug bites, swollen, itchy eyes, and vaginal discomfort. In addition, a strong chamomile rinse can add blonde highlights to light hair. For deep relaxation, add a quart of strong chamomile tea to a soothing bath. Soak for only 20 minutes if you have things to do, longer if you are going to bed afterwards. Dried chamomile flowers can also be added to moth-repelling mixtures in sachet bags along with lavender, wormwood, mugwort, and other herbs.

Chamomile has a long history of usage and is Generally Regarded As Safe (GRAS). However, chamomile belongs to the Asteraceae family, to which a small percentage of the population may be allergic. In addition, while it has been consumed safely for millennia during pregnancy, some obstetricians have recently added chamomile to a long list of herbal teas to avoid for fear of miscarriage in at-risk pregnancies.

Basic Chamomile Tea

For a pleasant cup of chamomile tea, steep for 3 to 5 minutes, then strain. When Mrs. Rabbit dosed Peter Rabbit after his foray into Mr. MacGregor's garden, she no doubt steeped it at least 10 minutes to settle his stomach and nerves. Honey, long known for its own healing qualities, may be added as desired.

Standard cup. 1 serving

1 tablespoon dried chamomile flowers
1 cup boiled water

Let the chamomile steep in the water for 3 to 5 minutes. Strain and sip slowly, inhaling its pleasant fragrance as you relax and contemplate your day.

Chamomile Tea Tisanes

Chamomile mixes well with other herbs for both pleasure teas and medicinal teas. Experiment with the ones you enjoy or try a few of the following.

Kids' Blend

I had a version of this tea at the 2024 Plant Cunning Conference in Central New York and it tasted good to both grownups and children. Lemon balm hydrates and eases sore muscles, fennel adds sweetness and eases digestion while catnip and chamomile add flavor as well as gentle calming.

2 to 4 servings, depending on the size of your teapot

1/2 teaspoon dried catnip
1 teaspoon dried chamomile
1 generous teaspoon dried or fresh fennel seed, bruised slightly
1 to 2 teaspoons dried or fresh lemon balm

In a small teapot or quart jar, pour boiling water over the herbs and allow to steep for 15 to 20 minutes. Strain and sip.

Feel Better Tea

Chamomile and peppermint work wonders together if you're tired but need to work a bit longer on something or go to a meeting and take notes. Chamomile can relax tense muscles while peppermint can perk you up and keep you focused. Both herbs figure strongly in Sleep Tea blends, for adding flavor and supporting the body to relax. If you're not feeling well or recovering from the flu or covid, this tea may help you to rest and fret less about what didn't get done while you were ill. Aromatic peppermint may also help restore your appetite.

Standard cup. 1 serving

1 teaspoon dried chamomile flowers
1 teaspoon dried peppermint leaves
1 cup of barely boiling water

Let the chamomile and peppermint steep in the water for 3 to 5 minutes. Strain and sip slowly, inhaling its pleasant fragrance.

Ease Me to Sleep, Please

Chamomile, catnip, catmint, and lemon balm collectively support restful sleep, ease tension and help the mind and body relax into a sleep-ready state. If you have not been sleeping well for quite a while, try drinking this tea with or shortly after dinner for a number of days. Note: it's probably best to drink it two to three hours before retiring, lest a full bladder undermine your efforts at undisturbed sleep.

2 to 4 servings, depending on the size of your teapot

1 tablespoon dried chamomile flowers
1/2 teaspoon dried catnip, catmint or lemon balm leaves
1/4 teaspoon lavender, optional

Pour boiling water over the herbs in a teapot and allow to steep for 10 minutes or more. Strain and sip.

Tummy Tea

Fennel seeds are useful for easing an upset stomach, especially with bloating or discomfort, but many of the Umbelliferae cousins—anise, coriander, caraway, and dill seeds—have been used to provide digestive relief as well. Coriander offers a citrus-like aroma and has been used to ease both simple stomach upsets and colic as well as the challenges associated with colitis, irritable bowel syndrome, Crohn's disease, and ulcerative colitis. **(Do consult your healthcare provider about any of these serious conditions.)** *Dill seed adds a wallop of calcium, anise a soft licorice flavor, and caraway a spicier tone, so choose the one whose flavor you like best. For added benefit, chew a few of the softened seeds. This tea also eases the symptoms of coughs and colds.*

2 to 4 servings, depending on the size of your teapot

1 tablespoon dried chamomile flowers
1 tablespoon dried fennel seeds, bruised

Pour boiling water over the herbs in a teapot and allow to steep for 15 minutes or more. Strain and sip.

Tummy Tea II

Chamomile eases digestion and relaxes tension while yarrow tones the intestinal tract. This tea may alleviate a variety of tummy troubles. Add honey, if desired.

2 to 4 servings, depending on the size of your teapot

1 to 2 teaspoons dried chamomile
1 scant tablespoon dried yarrow

In a small teapot or quart jar, pour boiling water over the herbs and allow to steep for 15 to 20 minutes. Strain and sip.

Anger Management Tea

When life is unfair and you're madder than you should be, try an herbal solution. Skullcap helps lower the level of anger, passionflower helps to stop replaying it in your head, while blue vervain and chamomile help to reduce stress and support relaxation. According to Matthew Wood, chamomile is especially helpful for cranky, whining, complaining, demanding folks. You can also add a quart of this tea to bathwater for additional support and relaxation.

2 to 4 servings, depending on the size of your teapot

1 teaspoon dried chamomile flowers
1 teaspoon dried blue vervain
1 teaspoon dried skullcap
1/2 teaspoon dried passionflower

In a small teapot or quart jar, pour boiling water over the herbs and allow to steep for up to 30 minutes. Strain and sip half a cup at a time.

Love and Romance Tea

When the stress and tension of a busy life get in the way of libido, try tis tea. Chamomile can help us relax; damiana, a Mexican desert plant, may put you in a romantic mood, and both pansy and roses are reputed to open the heart to love.

2 to 4 servings, depending on the size of your teapot

1/2 teaspoon dried chamomile flowers
1/2 teaspoon dried damiana leaves
1/2 teaspoon dried pansy flowers
1/2 teaspoon dried rose petals
Honey, optional

In a small teapot or quart jar, pour boiling water over the herbs and allow to steep for 15 to 20 minutes. Strain and enjoy with a hint of honey.

Achy Muscles and Cramp Tea

Bay leaves are an underused and underappreciated medicinal aid. Many Italian grandmothers have told me they give bay tea to their granddaughters "for the cramp." Historically, American colonists drank bay tea to alleviate back pain. Chamomile has long been used to soothe irritability and aid tense or strained muscles.

2 to 4 servings, depending on the size of your teapot

1 tablespoon dried chamomile flowers
1 small dried bay leaf, or 2 fresh, broken into pieces

Pour boiling water over the herbs in a teapot and allow to steep for at least 15 minutes. Strain and pour into a cup. Sip slowly, a quarter cup at a time.

Garden-grown chamomile should be mulched to retain soil moisture in hot weather; wheat-straw mulch used here. *Susan Belsinger*

Rapid Defense Tea

If you feel a cold or flu coming on, try this tea to prevent or diminish the symptoms at the start. Add honey, if desired.

2 to 4 servings, depending on the size of your teapot

1 teaspoon dried chamomile
1 teaspoon dried elderflower
1 teaspoon dried peppermint
1 teaspoon freshly grated ginger root or 1/2 teaspoon chopped crystallized ginger
1/2 teaspoon dried yarrow flower and leaf

In a small teapot or quart jar, pour boiling water over the herbs and allow to steep for 15 to 30 minutes. Strain and sip.

Chamomile-Ginger-Lemon Tea

Drink this tea for the sheer pleasure of it but if you are feeling under the weather, it might help you feel better, and hydrated too. The lemon offers a dose of vitamin C, depleted when we are under stress. Add honey, if desired.

2 to 4 servings, depending on the size of your teapot

1 teaspoon dried chamomile
1 teaspoon freshly grated ginger or 1/2 teaspoon chopped crystallized ginger
1/2 teaspoon fresh lemon juice or lemon zest

In a small teapot or quart jar, pour boiling water over the herbs and allow to steep for 15 to 20 minutes. Strain and sip.

Long Term Defense Tea

Tulsi, also known as Holy or Sacred Basil (Ocimum sanctum, O. gratissimum, O. tenuiflorum), is an adaptogen from Southeast Asia that helps us weather long term stress. Widely used in Ayurvedic medicine, tulsi has a distinctive aroma and sweet spicy flavor that goes well with chamomile which can ease short term stress. Try them together, with a slice of lemon for flavor and a dab of honey.

Standard cup. 1 serving

1 teaspoon dried chamomile
1 teaspoon dried tulsi

In a small teapot or quart jar, pour just boiled water over the herbs and allow to steep for 3 to 5 minutes, or to desired taste. Strain and sip.

Scottish Shortbread with Chamomile and Pistachios. *Gert Coleman*

Chamomile Cookies

What is tea without a good cookie? In herb school, we tried many different herbal teas, assessing taste, bitterness, healing qualities, and use in combinations. I quickly learned that eating a cookie with an herbal tisane that I wasn't nuts about helped it go down easily. Chamomile tea, in all of the above iterations, tastes very good with cookies, cakes, scones, and muffins. Chamomile itself tastes rather good in baked goods, too.

Scottish Shortbread with Chamomile and Pistachios

This was my mother's recipe for shortbread to which I often add herbs (thyme, dill, lemon zest) with a handful of chopped nuts. Serve in the pan, family-style, breaking off pieces as you go. Dried chamomile flowers combine very nicely with pistachios.

2/3 cup butter, at room temperature
1/2 cup sifted confectioners' sugar
1 1/2 cups plus 2 tablespoons sifted flour
1/2 teaspoon salt
1 to 2 pinches dried chamomile flowers, crushed
1/4 cup chopped pistachio nuts

Preheat oven to 325°F. Cream butter and sugar together until light and fluffy. Sift flour and salt into the creamed mixture and blend thoroughly by hand or with a wooden spoon. Press mixture into a nine-inch pie plate and pinch edges to form a pretty fluted rim.

Sprinkle nuts and chamomile flowers over the dough, pressing in lightly. Prick surface with a fork to mark 16 to 18 wedges. Bake until firm and lightly golden but not browned, about 45 minutes. Cool in pan.

Chamomile Shortbread Cookies

If you prefer your chamomile baked into the cookie, try this version. Add ginger for a warmer, holiday-season cookie. Chamomile combines well with both citrus and ginger in baked goods.

1 cup butter, at room temperature
1/2 cup granulated sugar
1/4 teaspoon salt
Zest of half an orange
1/2 teaspoon chopped crystalized ginger or freshly grated ginger, optional
1 heaping teaspoon dried chamomile, lightly crushed
2 1/2 cups flour

Preheat oven to 325°F. In a large mixing bowl, combine the butter, sugar and salt. Beat until light and fluffy. Blend together the orange zest, chamomile flowers, ginger if using, and flour. Stir into butter-sugar mixture, mixing until a smooth dough is formed. Press into nine-inch pie pan, pinching the edges.

Bake about 30 minutes, until golden or lightly browned. Remove from oven and let cool 5 to 10 minutes. Gently cut into 12 wedges. Allow to cool, then remove from pan.

Cold Chamomile Beverages: Cocktails and Mocktails

Chamomile tea can also be served iced, alone or with fruit juice and a dash of cinnamon. Add a jigger of your favorite alcohol. Experiment and create a new cocktail.

Chamomile syrup can be used to flavor many drinks and improve smoothies; be poured over ice cream, oatmeal, and pancakes; and, diluted, was long used to ease the irritation of infant teething. Any leftover syrup can be stored in the fridge.

Chamomile syrup appeals to mixologists as a good base for mocktails and cocktails. In addition, chamomile is a key flavoring in vermouth and an important ingredient in Manzanilla sherry and other digestive aperitifs. Chamomile was used in making beer during the Middle Ages, and sometimes as a substitute for hops in special brews today.

Chamomile Syrup

Makes 1 1/2 cups

1 cup sugar
1 cup water
3 individual organic chamomile tea bags or 1 heaping tablespoon dried
chamomile flowers

Place sugar and water in small saucepan and set over medium heat. Simmer,
stirring until sugar has dissolved. Remove from heat; add the chamomile tea
bags or dried flowers. Steep 10 minutes then discard tea bags. If using loose
chamomile, strain into container. Allow syrup to cool to room temperature,
then transfer to a clean jar with an airtight lid, and store in fridge for up to
two weeks.

Chamomile Lemonade

*You will need about 6 to 8 lemons for this lemonade. Add 1 ounce gin or
vodka for a refreshing cocktail.*

2/3 cup chamomile syrup
2/3 cup freshly squeezed lemon juice
3 cups water
Lemon slices for garnish

In a pretty glass pitcher, stir together chamomile syrup and lemon juice. Add
3 cups water, or more to taste. Chill and serve. Garnish with a few fresh
lemon or lime slices, or float a few fresh chamomile flowers on top.

Chamomile Lemon-Lime Rickey

When the world is altogether too much, perhaps the best thing to do is take a few minutes to relax with a soothing chamomile cocktail. You can use just lemon or just lime juice, but I like the two together. Float a few slices of lemon and lime, or some fresh chamomile flowers if you have them, in the glass. For a delicious and refreshing summer mocktail, skip the alcohol and garnish with a few circles of black Bing cherries or whole raspberries threaded onto a yarrow stem.

1/2 cup freshly squeezed lemon and lime juice, plus more to taste
2 to 3 tablespoons chamomile syrup
6 to 8 ounces seltzer water
1 to 2 ounces gin
Thin citrus slices or fresh chamomile flowers for garnish

Combine lemon and lime juice and chamomile syrup in a large glass. Stir and taste, adding more juice or syrup as needed. Add gin, fill with ice, add seltzer, and gently mix to combine. Add garnish.

References

Arrowsmith, Nancy. *Essential Herbal Wisdom: A Complete Exploration of 50 Remarkable Herbs*. Llewellyn, 2009. 333-342.

Groves, Maria Noel. *Herbal Remedies for Sleep*. Storey, 2024.

Mansefield, Katherine. "Camomile Tea." *All Poetry*. https://allpoetry.com/Camomile-Tea. Accessed 8/1/2024.

Potter, Beatrix. *The Tale of Peter Rabbit*. 1901. https://americanliterature.com/author/beatrix-potter/short-story/the-tale-of-peter-rabbit/. Accessed 9/13/24.

"Plants in Shakespeare." Candy, Melissa and Eddie Johnston. *Royal Botanic Gardens: Kew*. 22 April 2022. https://www.kew.org/read-and-watch/plants-in-shakespeare. Accessed 8/28/24.

Kowalchik, Claire and William H. Hylton, eds. *Rodale's Illustrated Encyclopedia of Herbs*. Rodale Press, 1987. 79-82.

Stewart, Amy. *The Drunken Botanist*. Algonquin Books, 2013. 205.

"Thinking with your Nose: Plants and the Perfume Industry." Chelsea

Physic Garden Company, 1996. 12.

Wood, Matthew. *The Earthwise Herbal*. North Atlantic Books, 2008. 177-182.

A writer, naturalist, and herbalist, **Gert Coleman** teaches nature writing workshops in the wild places of New York State and beyond.

Wild chamomile growing in the steps at James Duke's Green Farmacy Garden. *Susan Belsinger*

Cooking with Chamomile

Pat Crocker

As the beloved storyteller Beatrix Potter explained in *The Tale of Peter Rabbit*, circa 1902, chamomile soothes and pampers the body inside and out. After sipping a calming cup of chamomile tea, you can remove and chill the tea bags so that when the chamomile nudges you to take a nap, gently pat the chilled tea bags over closed eyes to ease inflammation and dark circles. Combining chamomile with lavender in a hot bath can be enough to encourage sleep after toweling off.

Traditional use of German chamomile (*Matricaria recutita*) has been for calming anxiety, assisting sleep, and to ease stomach aches. Both German and Roman chamomile (*Chamaemelum nobile*) have been used to treat heartburn, nausea, gas and vomiting thanks to the phytonutrient *coumarin* along with *eupatuletin* and *quercimethrin* flavonoids that give chamomile its antispasmodic and mildly sedative effects.

Brilliant blue *azulene,* a constituent that appears in the process of distilling chamomile essential oil, eases skin rash, insect bites, mild eczema and other minor irritations when applied to the skin in a carrier oil or cream. Medical herbalists and aromatherapists use the essential oil of German and Roman chamomile as a grounding, anti-depressant and sedative compound, and to reduce stress symptoms.

Fresh Chamomile in the Kitchen

M. recutita has a sweeter and more delicate taste than *C. nobile*, which is slightly more bitter, so I recommend that, for culinary use, German chamomile be used if possible.

The fresh flower is very aromatic, with a refreshing, green apple smell, which is why the fresh herb is often infused in apple juice. Unlike other flowers where the centers are discarded, the fragrant, bright yellow centers of chamomile blooms are also used along with the petals. Once you have infused and strained the juice, be sure to use it immediately or refrigerate it and use within 2 days.

Fresh Chamomile Infusion in Apple Juice

Having a chamomile-infused tisane available will inspire you to substitute it for water or other liquid in many of your favorite recipes. Try Chamomile Infusion in Apple Jelly; as the liquid for Risotto; breakfast Oatmeal; baked goods such as Oatcakes or Scones; and in Apple Ice Cream.

For ice cream and other cream desserts or puddings such as Panna Cotta, use a mixture of half Chamomile Infusion and half heavy cream (36% milkfat)—if you use low-milkfat milk or cream lower than 30% milkfat, the tisane will dilute the milk and the resulting product will be more like ice milk than ice cream.

Of course, freshly pressed apple juice is my first choice and if you use a commercial, tinned juice, try to find one with little or no sugar. You can use water in place of the apple juice for the tisane but the resulting liquid will not be as sweet or as 'apple-tasting' as one made with apple juice. This recipe may be doubled or tripled and frozen.

Makes 1 cup of Chamomile Infusion

1 cup apple juice
1/3 cup fresh chamomile flower heads

Heat juice in a small pot over medium-high heat until bubbles form around the sides of the pan.

Combine chamomile with heated juice in a teapot. Cover (and put a cork in the spout if possible) and steep for 2 hours, stirring occasionally, or overnight. Strain and use the cooled liquid immediately or strain into a jar with tight-fitting lid and refrigerate and use within 2 days.

Chamomile is included as an important food ingredient at a market in Cusco in the Peruvian Andes. *Pat Crocker*

Carrot Cake with Chamomile-Cream Cheese Icing

For convenience, this cake is baked in one 13 x 9-inch baking pan but you can use 2 cake pans for a round, layered cake. For a round, layered cake, you may need to make more icing or you can use Apple-Chamomile Jelly or Marmalade Jam for the filling.

Makes 24 2-inch square servings

Cake

2 cups all-purpose flour
2 teaspoons baking powder
2 teaspoons ground cinnamon
1/2 teaspoon salt
4 large eggs
1 1/2 cups granulated sugar
1 1/4 cups extra-virgin olive oil
3 cups shredded carrots
1 cup coarsely chopped pecans

Grease and lightly flour one 9 x 13-inch baking pan. Preheat oven to 350°F.

Combine flour, baking powder, cinnamon, and salt in a large mixing bowl. Stir with a fork to blend evenly and set aside.

Beat eggs and sugar together in a medium-size mixing bowl, using electric or hand beaters. Slowly beat oil into the egg-sugar mixture.

Drizzle about 1/2 cup of egg mixture over dry ingredients and beat with an electric beater. Add remaining wet ingredients, beating into the batter until well combined.

Stir in carrots and pecans and mix with a wooden spoon until well incorporated into the batter. Scrape batter into prepared pan.

Bake in preheated oven for about 40 minutes or until a cake tester (or toothpick) inserted into the center of the cake comes out clean. Set aside on a cooling rack for at least 10 minutes and turn out onto the rack to cool completely.

Icing

1/3 cup butter, room temperature
8 ounces cream cheese, room temperature
3 tablespoons Fresh Chamomile Infusion in Apple Juice (p. 106)
3 to 4 cups confectioners' (icing) sugar
1 cup coarsely chopped pecans, optional
12 whole pecan halves

Beat butter, cream cheese, and Chamomile Infusion together in a medium-size bowl using hand or electric beaters. Beat in 3 cups of sugar and test for consistency. If the icing is thin and runny, beat in more sugar until the icing is creamy and spreadable. Stir in chopped pecans if using.

Frost the cooled cake and decorate with whole pecan halves if using.

Fresh Chamomile Dressing

The chamomile and honey make this a versatile dressing for green salad, vegetables, or fruit, and it makes a light sauce for grilled fish.

Makes about 1/3 cup

1/4 cup extra virgin olive oil
2 tablespoons fresh chamomile flowers
3 tablespoons fresh lemon or lime juice
1 tablespoon liquid honey
Salt to taste

Combine oil, chamomile, citrus juice, and honey in a clean jar with tightly fitted lid. Cap, shake well, taste and add salt as required.

Use immediately or store in the refrigerator for up to 1 week. Bring to room temperature before using.

Jane Hawley Stevens harvests fresh chamomile at Four Elements Organic Herbals in New Freedom, Wisconsin. *Pat Crocker*

Dried Chamomile in the Kitchen

When dried, the flavor of chamomile is strong, green and herbaceous. However, some people—likely those who, like me, are also averse to cilantro—describe the taste of dried chamomile as cloying or soapy.

Dried chamomile is commonly used in herbal tea blends and in liqueurs. Because I don't like the cilantro-like taste of dried chamomile, I only use it fresh but the dried flower heads can be added to salads, desserts and other dishes as you would calendula. As with fresh chamomile, you can add chamomile's aroma and flavor to dishes by first making a strong tea and, just as you would with the Fresh Chamomile Infusion above, substitute it for the liquid ingredient in the recipe.

How To Dry Chamomile

Place whole chamomile flower heads in a dark, well-ventilated cupboard, and dry them slowly, to preserve their healing properties. If you can use a dehydrator, dry chamomile flower heads at 90°F for the first 24 hours, followed by a reduced temperature of 75 to 80°F for as long as it takes for the centers and petals to lose all trace of moisture.

If using a microwave oven, place flower heads in a single layer on a paper towel-lined shallow dish and dry on low to medium power for 2 minutes. Turn heads over and microwave for another 2 to 3 minutes. Keep turning and microwaving for about 6 to 20 minutes, or until flower heads are very dry.

Transfer to dark-colored, airtight, glass jars with tight-fitting lids. Label and store for up to 1 year in a dark place.

Dried Chamomile Tea

Because the taste of dried herbs is much stronger than that of the fresh, use the following rule of thumb for using dried chamomile in teas and recipes: 1 part dried herbs for every 3 parts fresh herbs. Keep in mind that the longer the tea steeps, the stronger and possibly more bitter the tea will become.

Chamomile in the drying chamber at Four Elements Organic Herbals, Wisconsin. *Pat Crocker*

Makes 4 cups of Chamomile tea.

4 cups water
2 to 3 tablespoons dried chamomile flower heads

Bring water to a boil in a kettle or pan over high heat. Pour over chamomile in a teapot or medium bowl. Cover tightly and steep for 2 hours, stirring occasionally, or overnight. Strain and use the cooled liquid immediately or strain into a jar with tight-fitting lid and refrigerate and use within 2 days.

Black Ginger-Chamomile Marmalade

If you are looking for a condiment that is different, this is it. I've adapted it from my book, *Preserving: the canning and freezing guide for all seasons* (see References). As with most spectacular things, it comes with a bit more work, but it is so worth it, especially if you like ginger. The color alone is stunningly unique for a preserve.

Unless you live in the tropics, fresh local ginger is probably not widely available, although it can be grown as an annual in places where the summers are long and warm (see References for a source for fresh, young ginger).

Crystallized or candied ginger and stem ginger in syrup are generally easy to find and store. Stem ginger is the term for the pink, tender stems growing out of the root and if available, use it for this recipe. If, like me, you can only find the woodier fresh gingerroot, use only the flesh surrounding the fibrous core but not the core itself. In the recipe, I am assuming that you will be using fresh gingerroot but if you are using stem ginger packed in syrup or crystallized ginger or candied ginger, measure 1 1/4 cup chopped and proceed to step 2.

Makes 4 cups

1 pound fresh gingerroot, peeled (see above)
4 cups Dried Chamomile Tea (recipe above)
4 cups fresh or frozen blackberries
1/2 cup freshly squeezed lemon juice
4 cups granulated sugar
1 pouch (3 oz/90 g) liquid pectin

Grate enough of the tender outer layer of the gingerroot to obtain 1 to 1 1/4 cups, lightly packed. In a saucepan, combine ginger with 4 cups water and bring to a boil over high heat. Boil for 5 minutes, drain and return ginger to the saucepan. Cover with 4 cups cold fresh water and repeat the boiling and draining twice so that the ginger has been boiled a total of 3 times. Drain well after final boiling. (The discarded water can be mixed with honey and lemon for tea or added to the compost.)

In a Maslin pan or large saucepan, combine ginger with Dried Chamomile Tea. Bring to a boil over high heat. Lower the heat and simmer gently until the shreds of ginger are tender and translucent, about 1 hour.

Meanwhile, in a bowl, mash the blackberries using a potato masher. Press through a cone sieve or coarse sieve lined with cheesecloth to remove the seeds, allowing the juice to collect in a non-reactive bowl or pan. Squeeze the cheesecloth to remove as much liquid as possible, discard cheesecloth and seeds. You should have about 1 1/3 cups blackberry juice.

Bring a large canner of water to a boil. Turn off heat and immerse four 1-cup jars in boiled water until the marmalade is ready. Scald the lids, jar lifter, funnel and tongs by placing in a shallow dish and covering with boiling water.

When the ginger is tender and translucent, drain well (saving liquid for another use) and add the blackberry juice and lemon juice and bring to a boil. Stir in sugar, one cup at a time, stirring until dissolved before adding the next cup. Bring to a hard boil and stir in the pectin. Boil, stirring constantly for 1 minute.

Skim and discard any foam. Fill hot jars, leaving a 1/4-inch headspace. Run a thin non-metallic utensil around the inside of the jar to allow air to escape. Add more hot marmalade if necessary, to leave a 1/4-inch headspace. Wipe rims, top with flat lids and screw on metal rings. Return jars to the hot water bath, topping up with hot water if necessary. Bring to a full rolling boil and process jars for 10 minutes.

Remove canner lid and wait 5 minutes before removing jars to a towel or rack to cool completely. Check seals, label and store in a cool place for up to 1 year.

Use: I like this purple-black marmalade on savory meats and both savory and sweet breads, but it can be used as a topping for puddings, ices and other desserts. It is especially delicious with cheesecake and yogurt and mixed with fresh fruits as a sweet dressing.

Powdered Chamomile

You can also powder dried chamomile flower heads and whisk into liquids or add to dry ingredients in recipes. Add powdered chamomile to spice blends, puddings, egg and cream dishes, in soup, dressings and sauces. Sprinkle over salads and vegetable dishes as a garnish.

To powder dried chamomile flower heads:

Use an electric spice grinder, small food processor, or mortar and pestle to pulverize them. Note that using a mortar and pestle produces a much coarser product than that produced by using an electric grinder or processor. Using a fine-wire mesh sieve, sift pulverized flower heads into a bowl and transfer to a dark-colored, glass jar. Tighten the lid, label, and store in a dark, dry place for up to 1 year.

Dried rose and calendula petals, lavender and clove pink petals may also be powdered.

Chamomile-Cinnamon Spice Blend

Use 2 teaspoons of this blend in place of the cinnamon in the Carrot Cake (p. 108) and most other recipes where cinnamon is called for. It blends easily into smoothies, puddings, dressings, and other sweet recipes where a hint of apple would be welcome.

You can also mix 1 teaspoon of this blend with 1 tablespoon liquid honey as a delicious sweetener for regular hot tea.

Makes 1/2 cup

1/4 cup dried, powdered chamomile flower heads
2 tablespoons dried, powdered cinnamon
2 teaspoons dried, powdered allspice berries
1 teaspoon dried, powdered cardamom seeds
Pinch dried, powdered cloves

Combine all ingredients in a small bowl and whisk with a fork to blend well. Transfer to a dark-colored, glass jar. Tighten the lid, label, and store in a dark, dry place for up to 1 year.

Bottom Line: Grow chamomile and use it in your kitchen and your apothecary.

References

Bremness, Lesley. *Essential Herbs*, London: Quadrile Publishing, 2000.

Crocker, Pat. *Preserving*. Toronto: HarperCollins Publishing, 2011.

Crocker, Pat. *The Herbalist's Kitchen*. New York: Sterling Publishing, 2018.

Young, fresh ginger: www.oldfriendsfarm.com

Pat Crocker's mission in life is to write with insight and experience, cook with playful abandon, and eat herbs with gusto. She is happiest when sharing what she knows about herbs, whole foods, and eating to be healthy.

As a professional Home Economist (BAA, Toronto Metropolitan University) and Culinary Herbalist, Pat's passion for healthy food is fused with her knowledge and love of herbs. She has honed her wellness practice over more than five decades of growing, photographing, and writing about what she calls, *the helping plants*. In fact, Crocker infuses the medicinal benefits of herbs in every original recipe she develops.

An award-winning author—she received the Herb Society of America Award for Excellence in Herbal Literature—Pat has written 23 herb/healthy cookbooks, including *The Herbalist's Kitchen*, *The Healing Herbs Cookbook*, and *The Juicing Bible*.

www.patcrocker.com @pc1writes

Decadent Chamomile Honey Cake. *Rosemary Davis*

Decadent Chamomile Honey Cake

Rosemary Roman Davis

The inclusion of rose water lends this cake a luxurious Persian note, which combines well with the fruity and wholesome nature of chamomile.

First, brew 1/2 cup strong chamomile tea, for both the cake and the syrup: (Use 1 heaping teaspoon of chamomile to 1/2 cup water; set aside to cool.)

Yield: 8 servings

1/4 cup plain yogurt, or almond milk
1/4 cup strong chamomile tea
1/3 cup all-purpose flour
1/3 cup whole wheat flour
1 cup almond flour
1 teaspoon baking powder
1/2 teaspoon ground cardamom
1 teaspoon salt
3/4 cup soft butter
1/3 cup sugar
1/4 cup honey
2 eggs, beaten
1/2 teaspoon pure vanilla extract
1/2 teaspoon pure almond extract

Grease an 8-inch round cake pan and line with parchment paper.

Preheat the oven to 350°F.

Whisk together the flours, salt, cardamom and baking powder.

Cream the butter and sugar together until fluffy, beat in the eggs, the extracts, 1/4 cup of the tea, and the yogurt or almond milk.

Fold the wet ingredients into the dry and mix just until smooth. Bake in the prepared pan for 45 minutes, or until lightly browned and a cake tester comes out clean.

Set the cake out to cool while you whisk together the syrup ingredients in a small bowl.

Chamomile Syrup

4 tablespoons honey
1/4 cup rose water
1/4 cup strong chamomile tea

If the honey is very viscous, warm the syrup ingredients over low heat in a small saucepan to dissolve completely. Pour the syrup over the warm cake (set it on a plate or tray to catch excess syrup) and let stand until cool.

Garnish with flowers, sliced almonds, or a sprinkle of confectioners' sugar.

Rosemary Davis bio on page 38.

Close up of dried *Matricaria recutita* tubular florets and hollow cones. *Susan Belsinger*

Chamomile Tipples

Karen England

Chamomile-Infused Apple Brandy

There is a Milton Berle quote that goes, "Every year my boss used to give me a bottle of expensive brandy because I'd told him that my doctor suggested a drink once in a while. This year my boss gave me the name of a new doctor."

I wanted to infuse apple brandy with chamomile to make a Chamomile-Infused Apple Brandy both for sipping and for making cocktails, but I found that there is a shortage of Apple Brandy in my area. I used to very easily be able to buy at my local liquor stores brandy and cognac which are made from grapes; Apple Brandy, Applejack and Calvados, which are brandies made from apples; Pear Brandy, made from pears and more. (The most recent pear brandy that I have owned was from Oregon a few years ago and the distiller grew pears in the bottles! Want to learn more about whole fruit in brandy bottles? Search online for the NPR The Salt article "Clear Fruit Brandies Pack an Orchard into a Bottle"). But lately apple brandy has been, and still is, unavailable.

So, since that was the case, I decided to use a regular, moderately priced grape brandy which is still readily available and infuse it with apples to make my own "apple brandy". I have done this before with great success but never with chamomile added. Now I will never be without this amazing and simple concoction. Each batch I make gets bigger to hopefully last longer…

This recipe can be scaled up or down as needed. (The basic formula is for every cup of brandy used, use one unpeeled, cored, cut-up apple and 1/8 cup of dried chamomile.) I use St. Remy XO French Brandy.

Yield: About 3 cups

Chamomile flowers and apples infusing in brandy. *Karen England*

1 750 ml bottle of brandy (250 ml =1 cup)
3 good-sized apples, (4 if they are small), use an assortment of varieties or
all one kind of apple—your choice—washed, cored, not peeled (peeled if
not organic), cut into 1/8ths (A medium-sized apple equals 1 cup diced.)
1/4 cup plus 1/8 cup dried chamomile

Combine all in a clean jar or jug (48 ounce) with a tight-fitting lid. Set aside
in a cool place for a month or longer. Full disclosure, I start using the brandy
within a week by using a ladle to remove an ounce or two from the jar before
sealing it back up and setting it aside to continue to macerate. After a month
or so, strain the brandy from the fruit and chamomile with a very fine mesh
strainer because some of the chamomile is quite tiny. Bottle and age it some
more if you are patient before enjoying neat or in cocktails. I'm not patient.
Just saying. Note: If some of the brandy is removed to enjoy sooner than one
month, the apples should be topped off with enough additional brandy to
keep them covered.

(Although I have not tried this—YET—pears can be substituted for the
apples in this recipe. According to *Better Homes and Gardens* "fruit math" for
bakers, 1 medium-sized pear equals 1 1/2 cups of diced pear and a medium-
sized apple equals 1 cup diced apple so I think using two pears per cup of
brandy and an 1/8 cup of chamomile would be sufficient to make a lovely
Chamomile-Infused Pear Brandy. I can't wait to try this!)

Manzanilla-Infused Brandied Apricots

Chamomile in Mexico is called *manzanilla*. This infused brandy is inspired
by the Mexican ice-pop treat called *Paletas de Chabacano y Manzanilla*
which translated is Popsicle of Apricot and Chamomile.

Whereas the apples were fresh in the brandy infusion above, the apricots are
dried in this infusion. This recipe is more about the apricots being brandied
than about the brandy itself although please don't misunderstand me—the
resulting brandy is delicious.

Yield: 1 cup

The formula for this version is 1/8 cup of dried chamomile per cup of dried
apricots.

Put both in a clean pint jar with a tight-sealing lid and cover completely with a moderately priced brandy. This recipe can be scaled up or down as needed. The difference from the apple-infused brandy is that I do not strain the brandy away from the apricots after this has been set aside for a while to steep. I keep them together and I use/eat the apricots which become quite plump for a delicious garnish/treat.

I also top off the jar with new brandy to keep the apricots that are still in the jar submerged as I use the contents. Because the apricots are dried, they soak up a lot of brandy and you end up with much less liquid than with the fresh apples.

Do you own Brandy Snifters? Did you get them for a wedding present or inherit them from your great Aunt Joan? So many people that I know who have brandy snifters have never used them and don't know why they should. You can drink brandy from any glass of course but according to *Eater.com*, "The snifter is specifically fashioned to enhance the sensory experience associated with sipping brandy, from first waft to final, warm sip."

Chamomile-Infused Apple Brandy. *Karen England*

Brandy snifters. *Karen England*

"A brandy snifter is a type of short-stemmed glassware specifically designed for drinking brandy and other liquors. It has a wide bottom and tapering top, which is designed to help concentrate the aroma of the drink for an enhanced tasting experience. The short stem allows the hand to warm the brandy, releasing its complex flavors and aromas" (www.definitions.net).

So, people, use your snifters!

If you don't have snifters but you do have stemmed wine glasses, just use those but instead of holding them by the stem so as to not warm the wine with your hands, hold the glass when drinking brandy in order to warm the drink in much the same way as it would in a brandy snifter.

Use the Chamomile-Infused Apple Brandy to make cocktails calling for apple brandy such as the Metropolitan which is really an inverted Brandy Manhattan. By that I mean that the ratio of vermouth to brandy is 2 to 1 in the Metropolitan cocktail instead of 1 to 2 as in a Brandy Manhattan. No bitters needed. Make either drink in a rocks glass or stemmed coupe and garnish with an apple slice.

Brandy Manhattan with Chamomile-Infused Apple Brandy and vermouth, garnished with lavender sprig and fresh chamomile flowers. *Karen England*

Metropolitan

Makes 1 serving

2 ounces vermouth (sweet or dry)
1 ounce Chamomile-Infused Apple Brandy
1 apple slice for garnish

Pour all ingredients into a mixing glass with lots of ice and stir 20 times or more. Strain into a chilled rocks glass and garnish with an apple slice.

Brandy Manhattan

Makes 1 serving

2 ounces Chamomile Apple-Infused Brandy
1 ounce vermouth (sweet or dry)
1 apple slice for garnish

Pour all ingredients into a mixing glass with lots of ice and stir 20 times or more. Strain into a chilled stemmed coupe glass and garnish with an apple slice.

Speaking of Vermouth … Why not make your own?

Real Deal Vermouth

I have an incomplete collection of 70 assorted issues of The Herb Grower Magazine ranging from April 1947 to Fall 1984. The collection has been cobbled together over the last 25 years and in the summer issue from 1970 George Gross wrote a column entitled "Vermouth II." (I don't have the spring 1970 issue, so I don't know what he wrote in "Vermouth I." There may have been a "Vermouth III" article in the winter 1970 issue, but I don't know since I don't have a copy of that either.) In "Vermouth II" George states that "vermouth is an unnatural product being made from fortified, acidulated and sweetened wines…" and he presents a table of twenty herbs in various combinations to produce a mild, mild-spicey, mild-herby or strong-bitter wine for a homemade sweet vermouth. His formulas make 1 to 2 gallons of vermouth, which is a lot even for me, so I only use his table for comparison with other vermouth recipes; namely my high school friend gave me his recipe for DIY vermouth that lacked so much information, even George couldn't help me. My friend's recipe goes like this: one bottle of white wine, one bottle of brandy, and one of sherry. Then a mix of herbs and spices. That's it!

So, using what George wrote in 1970 and my friend's bare bones recipe from 2019 I went googling do-it-yourself vermouth recipes and found one that seemed a good blend of the two on seriouseats.com. But that took a while. As you will read, this recipe that I am calling Real Deal Vermouth requires many ingredients and some time to age before drinking but is very worth the effort.

Makes approximately 4 1/2 cups

Zest of half a large unwaxed orange
3 1/4 cups white wine (such as a chardonnay), divided
1 large cinnamon stick
8 cardamom pods
3 fresh or dried bay leaves
1 star anise
1 teaspoon dried chamomile or 1 tablespoon fresh chamomile
1 teaspoon dried lavender or 1 tablespoon fresh lavender
1/4 teaspoon dried Sweet Annie leaf (*Artemesia annua*) or 1 teaspoon fresh Sweet Annie
1/4 cup sugar
1/4 cup boiling water
1/2 cup brandy
1/2 cup sweet sherry

Into a medium-size saucepan with a lid that we will call "pot A", pour 1 cup of the wine and add the orange zest and all the spices and herbs: cinnamon, cardamom, bay, star anise, chamomile, lavender, and sweet Annie and bring to a boil. Reduce the heat, cover and simmer 5 minutes. Remove pot A from the heat, strain out the herbs leaving only the wine and set aside to cool.

Put the sugar into a medium-large size saucepan, called "pot B", and cook on medium heat and stir approximately 5 minutes to caramelize. Remove from heat.

Being very careful, slowly pour 1/4 cup of boiling water into the caramel, stirring to combine.

Add the remaining wine to the herbal wine in pot A and bring back to a boil.

Off the heat, pour the boiling herbal wine in pot A into the caramelized sugar syrup in pot B and stir well. Stir in the brandy and sherry and cool completely before bottling and sealing.

Store in the fridge and age at least 1 week before using. Keep refrigerated and enjoy within several months.

Cheaters Chamomile Sweet Vermouth

In the meantime, while the Real Deal Vermouth was aging, I found a recipe in Emelie Tolley's book The Herbal Pantry for Chamomile Wine. This recipe called for 4 cups red or white wine, some chamomile fresh or dried, some orange and lemon peel and a bit of brown sugar ... however, chamomile wine just didn't appeal to me, so I moved on. Then, later, an idea hit me; what if I used Emelie's Chamomile Wine recipe to make chamomile vermouth instead?

So, I made two batches, one sweet and one dry, swapping out the red or white wine for sweet and dry vermouth. I followed Emelie's wine recipe exactly with both experiments and the Sweet Chamomile Vermouth recipe was the winner! Although the seriouseats.com DIY Sweet Vermouth Recipe was, in the end very good and included all my friend's few ingredients and many of George's numerous herbs, including chamomile, it just can't compete with the ease of making what I'm calling Cheaters Chamomile Sweet Vermouth inspired by Emelie Tolley.

Makes about 1 quart

4 cups sweet red vermouth, such as Gallo or Martini & Rossi
1/4 cup dried chamomile
1 tablespoon dried orange peel
1 teaspoon dried lemon peel
3 tablespoons dark brown sugar

Place all ingredients in a glass jar with a tight-fitting lid and steep in the refrigerator for up to a week before filtering and bottling. Note: All homemade vermouth should be refrigerated, and any open bottles of commercial vermouth should be stored in the refrigerator. The shelf life of opened or DIY refrigerated vermouth is 6 months.

Use either the Cheaters Sweet Chamomile Vermouth or the Real Deal Vermouth in most cocktail recipes calling for sweet vermouth such as The Slope Cocktail which is a Whiskey and Brandy drink attributed to Julie Reiner, Clover Club, New York. I'm calling my version the Slippery Slope.

The Slippery Slope

Makes 1 drink

2 ounces rye whiskey
3/4-ounce Cheaters Chamomile Sweet Vermouth
1/4-ounce Chamomile-Infused Apricot Brandy
2 dashes of bitters, such as Angostura or orange
1 brandied apricot, for garnish

Pour all ingredients into a mixing glass with lots of ice and stir 20 times or more. Strain into a chilled stemmed coupe glass and garnish with a brandied apricot.

And in conclusion, just a word of caution when making chamomile cocktails to not overdo it. For instance, using Cheaters Chamomile Sweet Vermouth in a cocktail with Chamomile-Infused Apple Brandy can be a bit too much. Although not a hard and fast rule, for the most part use the Cheaters Chamomile Sweet Vermouth or Real Deal Vermouth with plain brandy and other liquors in drinks, and use the Chamomile-Infused Apple Brandy with plain vermouth so that the chamomile sings, but doesn't overwhelm. Cheers!

References

"DIY Sweer Vermouth Recipe." https://www.seriouseats.com/how-to-make-red-vermouth-homemade-sweet-vermouth-recipe. Accessed 11-21-24.

www.eater.com/drinks/2015/6/12/8769503/getting-to-know-the-brandy-snifter-the-high-brow-glass-for-everyone Accessed 10-12-24.

www.azquotes.com/quote/964217?ref=brandy Accessed 10-9-24.

https://www.npr.org/sections/thesalt/2015/04/13/399348948/clear-fruit-brandies-pack-an-orchard-into-a-bottle Accessed 10-11-24.

https://www.definitions.net/definition/brandy+snifter

Ford, Adam. "Vermouth." *The Countryman Press*, 2015.

Regan, Gary. *The Joy of Mixology.* Clarkson Potter, 2018.

Tolley, Emelie. *The Herbal Pantry.* Clarkson N. Potter, 1992.

Karen England bio on page 44.

Chamomile ~ Herb of the Year 2025™

Ode to Chamomile

Apple scented with a hint of bitter,
You soothe my soul, my pain, my insomnia,
Chamomile tea.

Gert Coleman

Kilkenny

Health &
Beauty

Relax and Chill Out herbal tea blend. *Susan Belsinger*

Chamomile Formulations

Susan Belsinger

Besides being a calming and relaxing herb, chamomile is also good for the skin. I've been using *Matricaria recutita* in the following formulas for years and they work well for me. I generally use the annual German chamomile, however its close relative pineapple weed (*Matricaria discoidea*) and the perennial Roman chamomile (*Chamaemelum nobile*) are all anti-inflammatory, antidepressant and relieve skin irritations.

Take Time Out for Herb Tea Blend

This is a tea that I have been making for years—the three basic herbs being lemon balm, tulsi and nettles—soothing herbs that help with stress and anxiety. It is my before bedtime beverage. The nettles are also mineral rich; I sometimes add milky oats and now chamomile, Herb of the Year 2025. I make this in large batches since I drink it almost every night in cool weather and I sell bags of the blend (it makes a lovely gift) at a few holiday markets.

Makes 4 cups tea blend; fills a quart jar

1 cup chamomile flowers
1 cup tulsi leaves and flowers
1 cup lemon balm leaves
1 cup nettle leaves

Combine whole leaves and flowers in a bowl and toss to mix. Transfer the herbal blend into a jar and label.

I use about 2 tablespoons of the blend to a generous cup of just-boiled water and let steep for at least 5 minutes. Sweeten with a tad of honey or maple syrup, if desired.

Nighty-Night, Sleep-Tight Bath Oil

I love to take baths and this synergistic blend will relax you and help with a good night's sleep. Use whatever oil you prefer or make a blend: almond, olive, jojoba, and/or avocado oil. If you don't have all five of the following essential oils, or don't like one of them, just leave it out and make it anyway.

Lavender—relaxing, uplifting, balancing and refreshing, blends well with other oils

Chamomile—good for skin care, gentle, soothing, warming and relaxing

Bergamot—refreshing and uplifting, balancing effect on emotions, warming

Hops—sedative, good for sleep and anxiety, soothing

Yarrow—helps heal rashes, wounds and inflammation, calming

Makes a 4 ounce bottle or about 1/4 cup

1/4 (4 ounces) cup carrier oil
8 drops lavender essential oil (*Lavandula angustifolia*)
6 drops chamomile essential oil (*Matricaria recutita*)
6 drops hops essential oil (*Humulus lupulus*)
6 drops bergamot essential oil (*Citrus bergamia*)
4 drops yarrow essential oil (*Achillea millefolium*)

Pour the carrier oil into a clean, dark glass bottle that has a dropper or an orifice reducer (removed to fill bottle); leave a little headspace. Carefully drop each essential oil into the bottle, cap and shake to blend. Label and keep in a cool place, out of direct sunlight.

After running the water into the tub, add 1 scant teaspoon of the oil to the bath and swish the floating oil into the hot water with your hand before submerging your body.

Azulene is the compound that lends the blue color to this lovely-scented massage or bath oil formula. *Susan Belsinger*

Blissful Blend Bath or Massage Oil

Many years ago, I came across a bath oil called bliss blend and I really liked the combination of fragrances—and how it made me feel—so I created my own version. I looked online and couldn't find it anywhere, however there were many other "bliss blend" products, although none of them were even vaguely similar to this blend. Use carrier oils of your choice—I like a combo of half almond oil and half olive oil.

Lavender—relaxing, uplifting, balancing and refreshing, blends well with other oils

Chamomile—good for skin care, gentle, soothing, warming and relaxing

Cedarwood—soothing and harmonious, warming and sensual

Clary Sage—warming, relaxing, uplifting, induces a sense of well being

Makes a 4-ounce bottle or about 1/4 cup

1/4 (4 ounces) cup carrier oil
8 drops lavender essential oil (*Lavandula angustifolia*)
6 drops chamomile essential oil (*Matricaria recutita*)
6 drops clary sage essential oil (*Salvia sclarea*)
6 drops cedarwood essential oil (*Cedrus atlantica, C. species*)

Pour the carrier oil into a clean, dark glass bottle that has a dropper or an orifice reducer (removed to fill bottle); leave a little headspace. Carefully drop each essential oil into the bottle, cap and shake to blend. Label and keep in a cool place, out of direct sunlight.

After running the water into the tub, add 1 scant teaspoon of the oil to the bath and swish the floating oil into the hot water with your hand before submerging your body.

Or use as a massage oil; dilute a little bit more with carrier oil (1 or 2 tablespoons) if the person being massaged finds this blend a bit too strong in fragrance.

Herb Potpourri Sugar Scrub

This is not edible—it is for your skin. Sugar cane produces glycolic acid, which is a natural alpha hydroxy acid that exfoliates the skin. This doesn't dry your skin out like a salt scrub does and will leave your skin feeling really soft and well lubricated. Use whatever combination of dried herbs you like—a combination of 2 or 3 is good—remove the leaves or flowers from stems. Essential oils may also be used, just be sure that they are pure oils and not chemically made. This recipe is excerpted from <u>the creative herbal home</u> by Susan Belsinger and Tina Marie Wilcox.

Besides being good for the skin, these herbs are soothing, anti-stressful, and uplifting.

Lavender—a cell regenerator and has the reputation for slowing wrinkles. It is used on scarring, burns, sun-damaged skin, stretch marks, rashes, and skin infections

Chamomile—good for all skin types and can be used to treat sensitive or puffy skin as well as rashes and enlarged capillaries

Calendula—heals skin wounds, rashes, inflammations, and bites; it is a natural cell regenerator

Basil—good for oily skin and sore muscles

Makes 8 ounces; about 1 cup

1 cup less 2 tablespoons cane sugar
About 2 ounces (4 to 6 tablespoons) olive, almond, grapeseed, or jojoba oil, or a combination thereof
1 to 2 tablespoons crushed dried herbs: organic dried lavender, chamomile flowers, calendula petals, basil leaves
1 teaspoon vegetable glycerin, optional
Few drops of essential oils such as lavender, basil or chamomile

Put the sugar in a non-reactive bowl. If using dried herbs, crush them with a mortar and pestle or pulse them in a spice grinder until finely chopped and add them to the sugar. Add the oil and glycerin. If using essential oils, drop them into the oil to disperse. Blend well, transfer into clean jars; use plastic lids. Label.

In the shower, scoop some scrub into your hand and gently massage it into

Although I tend to use tinctures rather than glycerites, Chamomile Glycerite is one to have on hand—great for kids and those who are avoiding alcohol.
Susan Belsinger

your skin. Leave for a minute or two and rinse with warm water. Sometimes after using, the sugar gets a bit hard from water getting mixed with it—just rub between your hands to crumble it and use as directed. When the scrub is just about gone, if there is still liquid and herbs in the bottom of the jar, add another scoop of sugar and shake the jar.

Caution: please be careful in shower when using oil, since it may be slippery. Gently pat dry. It is best not to use this for the first time before a special event in case the cleansing causes blotchy skin.

Warning: since each individual may react differently, if you have allergies or have not used these particular essential oils before, you should do a patch test by rubbing the scrub on the inner part of your elbow and waiting a few hours, before using all over your body or face. It is not safe to use many essential oils if you are pregnant or nursing, so research this carefully if you are. If you have any concerns or questions, contact your health care provider.

Chamomile Glycerites

Why make a glycerite? You may not want to give alcohol-based tinctures to your children or you might have an adult who does not tolerate or who is abstaining from alcohol. Other than alcohol, the best, shelf-stable menstruums are vegetable glycerin and apple cider vinegar. These are not quite as strong as alcohol tinctures, however they make a good, milder remedy for children and those who are avoiding alcohol.

In her blog on making glycerites, herbalist Kristine Brown describes exactly what a glycerite is: "Glycerin is a thick, clear, sticky liquid that is made from fat/oil and generally from soy, palm, or coconut oil though it can be made from animal and petroleum products as well, and is the sugar alcohol, known as glycerol or glyceric alcohol, from these products. It is created by heating the fat under pressure, often with an alkali such as lye, to cause the sugar alcohol to split away from the fatty acids."

Naturally sweet, kids usually will take glycerites. Making a glycerite is similar to making a tincture; it is a fairly stable menstruum with some medicinal, antiseptic and preservative properties and it does not evaporate.

This chamomile glycerite is a wonderful, gentle remedy to have on hand. It relieves upset stomach, colic, anxiety and helps with insomnia.

Fresh herb glycerite using the folk method

Rough chop the fresh herb and pack it into a measuring cup. For 1 cup of fresh chopped herb use 2 cups of vegetable glycerin. Transfer the herb to a blender and add just 1 cup glycerin. Blend the ingredients to combine well. Generally, with fresh botanicals, it is not necessary to add water, since there is already water in the herb leaves and flowers. If it is very thick—you can add 1 to 2 tablespoons of water to loosen it a bit.

Pour the blended herbal glycerin into a 2-cup jar and add about 1 cup more of glycerin—enough to fill the jar. Tightly cap and shake well. Label the jar and date. Keep out of direct sunlight and shake the glycerite every day for at least 2 and up to 6 weeks.

When ready to bottle the glycerite, it helps to gently heat the glycerite in a water bath to facilitate the straining process. Use a strainer lined with a piece of dampened muslin or cheesecloth and strain the glycerite into a bowl or wide-mouthed glass measuring cup. Pour the glycerite into the prepared strainer and let sit; this will take some time since the mixture is thick. Use a spoon to hurry up the process—or not—once most of the glycerin has passed through, gather up the corners of the cloth, twist them around the herbs and squeeze out the rest of glycerite.

Pour into small, dark glass, dropper bottles, close tightly and label with contents, method and date. James Green says that glycerites keep for 1 to 3 years and recommends refrigeration when possible.

Tieraona Low Dog's suggested dosage is 1 drop per pound of bodyweight up to 60 pounds, and then 1 teaspoon, 4 x a day for children 60 to 100 pounds. Teens and adults can take 1 tablespoon up to 4 x a day.

Dried herb glycerite using the folk method

When diluted, glycerin becomes emollient, demulcent, and healing.

When using dried herbs to make a glycerite, you will need to add some water to the glycerin and will need to grind or powder the herbs so they absorb as much of the menstruum as possible. You can use a mortar and pestle, high-speed blender or food processor to break down the dried herbs as much as possible. For a pint jar (2 cups) add 1 cup of prepared dried herbs—so it is about half full.

The general recommended amount of glycerin for a shelf-stable glycerite is 60% glycerin and 40% water. Glycerin contains about 5% water so this brings the amount of glycerin down to 55% and the water to 45%. Some herbalists prefer a higher percentage of 75% glycerin and 25% water, which yields about 70% glycerin/30% water, taking the water in the glycerin into consideration.

All that said, if you have 1 cup of powdered herb in your pint jar, you will want to mix 7/8 cup of glycerin with 2/3 cup water for a 60/40% blend. One cup glycerin to 1/2 cup water is about 66/34% blend and 1 1/8 cup glycerin to 1/3 cup water is about 75/25% blend.

The glycerin and water need to be combined and mixed thoroughly before adding to the dried herbs. Once mixed, about a third of the liquid menstruum can be added slowly to the powdered herb and mixed well so that the dried herbs are thoroughly moistened. Keep adding the menstruum, stirring as you go until nearly all of the liquid is added and the jar is full; pour the last bit of menstruum on top so that about 1/4-inch of it is above the herb glycerite.

Tightly cap and shake well. Label the jar and date. Let the jar sit overnight or for about 12 hours. If the herbs have absorbed all of the menstruum, add a floater of another 1/4-inch or so of glycerin on top. Keep out of direct sunlight and shake the glycerite every day for at least 2 and up to 6 weeks.

When ready to bottle the glycerite, it helps to gently heat the glycerite in a water bath to facilitate the straining process. Use a strainer lined with a piece of dampened muslin or cheesecloth and strain the glycerite into a bowl or wide-mouthed glass measuring cup. Pour the glycerite into the prepared strainer and let sit; this will take some time since the mixture is thick. Use a spoon to hurry up the process—or not—once most of the glycerin has passed through, gather up the corners of the cloth, twist them around the herbs and squeeze out the rest of glycerite.

Pour into small, dark glass, dropper bottles, close tightly and label with contents, method and date. James Green says that glycerites keep for 1 to 3 years and recommends refrigeration when possible.

Tieraona Low Dog's suggested dosage is 1 drop per pound of bodyweight up to 60 pounds, and then 1 teaspoon, 4 x a day for children 60 to 100 pounds. Teens and adults can take 1 tablespoon up to 4 x a day.

Chamomile bitters are not only tasty—they are wonderful for your digestion.
Susan Belsinger

Chamomile Bitters

Susan Belsinger

I am a bit of a bitters fanatic; I quite like them and make my own, as well as teach classes on how to make your own. One of my favorite commercial bitters is Calm Tummy Bitters made by Urban Moonshine. They are one of the first small craft bitters makers—I've been buying their products since they started selling them in 2008 and I highly recommend them. I have and use all of their bitters (I buy the 8-ounce size and refill my dropper bottles). Since chamomile is Herb of the Year and I use a lot of U.M. chamomile bitters, I decided to make my own version.

Their ingredient label lists: water, cane alcohol, dandelion root extract, dandelion leaf extract, chamomile flower extract, burdock root extract, yellow dock root extract and ginger root extract. I am using roots and flowers that I grew and dried, except the ginger rhizome is fresh chopped. The sweetener is optional—it rounds out the flavor—and cuts the bitterness slightly for those new to using bitters.

Yields 2 cups

1/4 cup dried chamomile flowers or 1/3 cup fresh flowers
2 tablespoons chopped dandelion root
1 heaping tablespoon dried hop flowers
1 heaping tablespoon chopped burdock root
1 heaping tablespoon chopped fresh ginger root
2 cups 100-proof vodka, or alcohol of your choice
1/2 cup non-chlorinated water
About 1 to 2 tablespoons honey, maple syrup or organic sugar, optional

Combine the prepared herbs and roots in a pint jar or bottle. Pour the alcohol over the botanicals to fill the jar and completely cover them. Cap the bottle or jar, label and date, and shake the container daily for 2 weeks. Open and taste the bitters. If you are happy with the strength and flavor, strain the menstruum from the marc; if you want it to be a bit stronger leave the botanicals in the menstruum and wait another week or two.

After straining the bitters, put them aside and put the marc into a small saucepan and cover with 1/2 cup water and bring to a simmer. Simmer gently for 10 minutes, checking that there is still liquid in the pan. Place a lid on the pan and let cool a bit; while still warm stir in 1 tablespoon sweetener—or 2 tablespoons if you prefer it sweeter. Strain the liquid from the marc and add it to the bitters; discard the marc to the compost.

Bottle the bitters, preferably in a dark glass bottle with a dropper, and label. Store in a cool dark place away from direct sunlight. Take one half dropperful about 1/2 hour before or after meals.

References

Belsinger, Susan and Tina Marie Wilcox. *the creative herbal home*. herbspirit, 2007.

Brown, Kristine. *Basic Folk Method of Making Glycerites.* https://herbalrootszine.com/. Accessed 7/6/2021.

Coleman, Gert, ed. *Hops, Herb of the Year 2018*. International Herb Association, 2018.

Connole, Kathleen, ed. *Yarrow, Herb of the Year 2024*. International Herb Association, 2024.

Green, James. *The Herbal Medicine Maker's Handbook*. Crossing Press, 2000.

Keville, Kathi and Mindy Green. *Aromatherapy: A Complete Guide to the Healing Art*. The Crossing Press, 1995.

Low Dog, Tieraona. *Healing Remedies: A Holistic Approach to Health and Wellness*. National Geographic, 2014.

https://www.bbg.org/article/weed_of_the_month_pineapple_weed. Accessed June 15, 2024.

Susan Belsinger bio on page 17.

Fresh chamomile should be wilted or dried before using in formulations. *Susan Belsinger*

The Bitter with the Sweet

Kathleen Connole

He who has not tasted bitter things, knows not what sweet is.
~ German proverb

Why are some herbs bitter? This biochemistry and that of other constituents in some very familiar and much-used herbs—such as chamomile—are said to have evolved to deter herbivores and other predators from eating them. During the study of *Yarrow Herb of the Year 2024,* the subject of bitter herbs became intriguing. How did humans figure out which bitter herbs were toxic, and which were beneficial?

Archeological discoveries of yarrow, *Achillea millefolium,* and chamomile, *Matricaria chamomilla,* in the dental calculus of Neanderthal era humans have led to the conclusion that these early people were using plants to self-medicate. Both herbs have a bitter taste and would not have been sought out as a source of nutrients.

Recognizing bitter taste as evidence of toxicity presents an evolutionary advantage, and scientific studies have shown that primates, including humans, know which bitter plants to avoid and which can be used as medicine. It stands to reason that if one member of a social group became ill or even dropped dead after consuming a certain plant, the others would avoid that behavior and pass on that knowledge.

Bitter herbs can be appetite suppressants due to the constituents dihydro-azulene, chamazulene, coumarin, and 4 methylherniarin (Hardy et al, 2012). They thus could have been of help during times of food shortages for hunter gatherers.

Chamomile Herb of the Year 2025 is a bitter herb that is well-known for the sweet fragrance and taste of its flowers. The tea made from chamomile flowers will become bitter when it is steeped longer than 15 minutes. The foliage of chamomile is bitter.

The article "The pharmacological activities of *Matricaria chamomilla* confirm its traditional uses" lists the plant's biological properties: antioxidant, antibacterial, antifungal, anti-parasitic, insecticidal, anti-diabetic, anti-cancer, and anti-inflammatory (Merah, ed., 2022).

Certain secondary plant compounds protect the plant from insects, parasites, and pathogens. These same qualities could be the reason that yarrow and chamomile are both known to be good companion plants. Observations made by several gardeners during our study of *Yarrow Herb of the Year 2024* seem to verify this.

Bitter plant constituents are rarely found alone; other beneficial properties that often occur along with them include anti-inflammatory, antimicrobial, immunomodulatory, and analgesic (Hart, 2005). Self-medicating with bitter herbs would aid in survival from disease and thus the ability to reproduce and raise young. There is a genetic predisposition for bitter taste receptors, which would be passed on.

In the study analyzing human bitter taste receptors, regarding plants with a strong versus a weak bitter taste, Zerbe suggests that "an elevated sensitivity would not necessarily be beneficial, but could lead to the rejection of edible food, which would be an evolutionary disadvantage" (Zerbe, ed., 2020). Chamomile is a good example of such an herb—the tea made from the flowers is usually only weakly bitter.

The taste of bitter herbs such as coffee and cacao is often made more palatable by adding cream and sugar. The ancient people of Central America, where cacao is native, added certain flowers and honey to make the frothy beverage that was served to royalty. Cacao was a regular part of Aztec soldiers' military rations; it was ground into pellets or wafers and issued to every soldier on a campaign (Coe, 98).

Some other examples of bitter-tasting beverages and foods are beer, wine, extra-virgin olive oil, certain aged cheeses, citrus, leaf lettuces, and cruciferous vegetables. The long-standing common practice of serving a dinner salad at the beginning, or ending, of a meal aids in digestion.

We know that the primary taste sensations are sweet, bitter, sour, salty, and umami. "Sweet taste enables the identification of energy-rich nutrients, umami enables the recognition of amino acids, salty taste ensures the proper balance of dietary electrolytes, and sour and bitter tastes warn about the ingestion of potentially harmful and/or poisonous chemicals" (Chandrashekar et al, 288).

The food industry typically aims to mask or minimize bitterness to increase acceptance of products "through selective [plant] breeding and a variety of debittering processes" (Drewnowski, 2000). However, removing or breaking down healthy bitter phytonutrients surely must reduce the beneficial effects attributed to some of these foods.

It seems that a preference for sweet and salty foods in the dietary choices of our modern world, coupled with an increasing aversion to bitter and sour flavors, can lead to poor nutrition and result in metabolic syndrome and its consequences—obesity, hypertension, diabetes, and neurodegenerative diseases. (In addition, digestive woes seem to be all too common, if one is to believe all the drug commercials on television continuously being promoted to treat them.) Prenatal experience and early exposure to foods high in energy, sugar, or fat can lead to a preference for these foods and an aversion to such foods as those in the cabbage family later in life. More than one study cited evidence that those with such an aversion eat 25 percent less vegetables, which can lead to a greater incidence of colon cancer.

German Zuluaga, who spent years in the Colombian Amazon with the Inga people, presents a very thorough discussion of his study of indigenous people and their use of herbs as medicine. He discovered that they determine the therapeutic value of plants by their taste and found that the bitter taste of plants was instrumental in understanding "the universe of indigenous and traditional therapeutics" (Zuluaga, 2010). He went on to determine the active phytochemicals in the plants used in their traditional medicine, which explains their therapeutic value as understood in the terms of Western medicine.

The science of bitter taste receptors in humans is still being studied and there are multiple articles available explaining the latest findings. Between 24 and 29 bitter taste receptors have been identified. These taste receptors are not limited to the oral cavity, "they are expressed in numerous tissues … and fulfill important roles in metabolic regulation, innate immunity and respiratory control" (Zuluaga, 2010).

Many folks drink chamomile tea medicinally for its digestive benefits:

> "When bitter constituents are tasted on the tongue, a reflex action occurs from the receptors (referred to as T2Rs) located on the taste buds. Thus, taste signals are transmitted to the brain. This initiates

the priming of digestive function through stimulating increased digestive secretions such as gastrin and pepsin, simultaneously increasing the motility of gallbladder and bile flow. Gastrin performs many actions: gastric acid and pepsin secretion; pancreatic digestive secretions; intestinal juice production; and cell division and growth of stomach, intestinal and pancreatic tissues ... Bitters also have a cooling property and can be applied to inflammatory states ... and are antibiotic, antifungal, antitumor, sedative, expectorant, and antimalarial. [They] also help the liver to self-clean and reduce toxic accumulations" (Zuluaga, 2010).

The principle bitter plant compounds are alkaloids, terpenoids, saponins, amino acids, and bitter peptides. Most plant metabolites are bitter: polyphenols, flavonoids, isoflavones, terpenes, glucosinolates (www. sciencedirect.com). The terpenoids bisoprolol, matricin, and chamazulene that are found in chamomile give it its bitter taste (Valduga, 2019).

Some familiar bitter plants and the parts used, listed in multiple studies, include quinine, *Cinchona calisaya, C. ledgeriana, C. officinalis, C. pubescens*, dried bark; Dutchman's pipe, *Aristolochia reticulata*, dried rhizome and roots; goldenseal, *Hydrastis canadensis*, dried rhizome and roots; barberry, *Berberis vulgaris*, bark and berries; gentian, *Gentiana lutea*, rhizome and root; Angostura, *Galipea officinalis*, dried bark; dandelion, *Taraxacum officinale*, fresh and dried root; Oak, *Quercus* spp., dried bark; tulip tree, *Liriodendron tulipifera*, bark; white turtlehead, *Chelone glabra*, fresh herb; bayberry, *Myrica cerifera*, bark and seeds; chamomile, *Chamaemelum nobile* and *Matricaria recutita,* herb; fringe tree, *Chionanthus virginicus*, root; wormwood, *Artemisia absinthium*, herb; taxus, *Taxus brevifolia*, bark; St. John's wort, *Hypericum perforatum*, dried aerial parts; bitter orange, *Citrus aurantium*, ripe fruit; white horehound, *Marrubium vulgare*, dried herb; tansy, *Tanacetum vulgare*, aerial parts; yarrow, *Achillea millefolium*, herb; and hops, *Humulus lupulus*, flower.

In one study, the constituents of 25 bitter herbs were analyzed for their therapeutic effects: 76% were found to be anti-inflammatory, 56% antimicrobial, 44% immunomodulatory, 28% analgesic; 96% were found to have one or more of these beneficial properties (Hart, 2018).

As the research was conducted for this article, my questions about the toxicity of bitter herbs were finally answered in the article "The Taste of Toxicity: A Quantitative Analysis of Bitter and Toxic Molecules" (Nissim et al, 2017).

In this extensive study of bitter compounds found in plants, the conclusion was that even though bitterness is often associated with poisons, it is not a strong indicator of high toxicity. The study states that "roughly two thirds of known bitter compounds have some level of toxicity, but less than 20% are in the fatal or toxic category ... [these] may be harmful only at concentrations unrealistically high for oral consumption" (Nissim et al. 2017).

Now, what about "bitters"?

According to a *Smithsonian* article "A Brief History of Bitters," author P. Smith tells us that the earliest bitters on the market were patent medicines of "dubious reputations" originally made from roots, barks, and spices. Angostura bitters are some of the oldest and are named for the Venezuelan city Angostura (renamed Cuidad Bolivar in 1846). Early botanists gave the name Angostura to three species of trees, including *Galipea officinalis*. It is unknown if the original formula contained the bark of any of these plants, but it seems likely. Angostura bitters are still being made and are very familiar for their use in cocktails; of course, the recipe is a tightly guarded secret.

We can easily make our very own bitters, and a recipe for Chamomile bitters can be found in Susan Belsinger's article on formulations in this book. You will notice that the recipe includes some sweetening to tame the bitter taste a bit.

As with any herbal remedy, we must first do our homework and determine which formulations will be most beneficial in treating the condition that we wish to address.

The School of Evolutionary Herbalism's website blog, "The Benefits and Dangers of Bitters," outlines the physiological responses to consuming bitters. The energetics of bitters include the well-known positive effects on the digestive system, due to the downward energetic motion that "tends to drain things down and out ... There can be an overall constitutional cooling and drying effect" over time (www. evolutionaryherbalism.com).

This can also be beneficial in treating inflammation and congestion of the respiratory system. However, if a person tends to be cold, warming herbs such as fennel, *Foeniculum vulgare*, or cloves, *Syzygium aromaticum*, can be added to the formulation of bitter herbs such as chamomile. If there are symptoms of dryness such as dry eyes or dry mouth, the bitter formulation should also contain a demulcent plant, such as marshmallow, *Althea officinalis*; licorice root, *Glycyrrhiza glabra;* or slippery elm*, Ulmus rubra* (www.evolutionaryherbalism.com).

All this to say, do not be afraid of the bitter herbs. Since my experience with using them, beginning with the study of the very bitter *Yarrow Herb of the Year 2024*, and now, *Chamomile,* I can personally attest to their benefits.

References

Behrens M, Ziegler F. "Structure-Function Analyses of Human Bitter Taste Receptors-Where Do We Stand?" *Molecules*. 2020 Sep 26;25(19):4423. doi: 10.3390/molecules25194423. PMID: 32993119; PMCID: PMC7582848. Accessed 12-11-24.

Chandrashekar, J. "The receptors and cells for mammalian taste." *Nature*, 2006. www.pubmed.ncbi.nlm.nih.gov. Accessed 1-3-25.

Coe, M., and S, Coe *The True History of Chocolate*. Thames & Hudson Ltd, London, 2013.

Drewnowski, A., Gomez-Corneros, C. "Bitter Taste, Phytonutrients, and the Consumer." *The American Journal of Clinical Nutrition,* Vol. 72, 2000. www.sciencedirect.com. Accessed 1-3-25.

Hardy, K., Buckley, S., & Collins, M. (2012). "Neanderthal medics? Evidence for food, cooking, and medicinal plants entrapped in dental calculus." *Naturwissenschaften,* 99(8), 617-626. Accessed 12-13-24.

Hart, B. "The Evolution of Herbal Medicine: Behavioral Perspectives." *Eleesevier Ltd.*, 2005. Accessed 10-31-24.

Merah, ed. "Chamomile (*Matricaria chamomilla* L.): A Review of Ethnomedical Use, Phytochemistry, and Pharmacological Uses." *Life (Basel),* 2022. www.pmc.ncbi.nlm.nih.gov. Accessed 1-3-25.

Nissim, I., Dagan-Wiener, A. and Niv, M.Y. (2017). "The taste of toxicity: A quantitative analysis of bitter and toxic molecules." *IUBMB Life*, 69: 938- Accessed 12-13-24.

Popham, Sajah. "The Plant Path: The Benefits and Dangers of Bitters." *The School of Evolutionary Herbalism*. www.evolutionaryherbalism. com/2021/04/28/the-benefits-and-dangers-of-bitters/. Accessed 12-13-24.

Valduga. A. "Chemistry, Pharmacology, and New Trends in Traditional, Functional, and Medicinal Beverages." *Food Research International*, 2019. www.sciencedirect.com. Accessed 1-3-25.

Zerbe, ed. "Structure-Function Analyses of Human Bitter Taste Receptors

– Where Do We Stand?" *Molecules*, 2020. www.pmc.ncbi.nlm.nih.gov. Accessed 1-3-25.

Zuluaga, G. "Potential of Bitter Medicinal Plants: A Review of Flavor Physiology." *Pharmaceuticals (Basel)*, 2024. www.pubmed.ncbi.nlm.nih. gov. Accessed 12-13-24.

Kathleen Connole bio on page 25.

Natural Beauty with Chamomile

Janice Cox

Every garden should have a small patch of chamomile growing somewhere. It is a great companion plant that helps other plants thrive and grow around it. An old belief is that chamomile was the garden's doctor. When planted near sick or dying plants, it seemed to cure them and make them grow again.

It also can be used in body care products keeping your skin and hair naturally beautiful. Chamomile is an all-around beauty herb used in creams, lotions, toners, and many hair products. You cannot beat this popular herb for its gentle nature and effectiveness at calming a complexion breakout.

Chamomile has been used for centuries to calm and beautify the skin. Ancient Egyptians valued chamomile for its healing properties and used it in a variety of skin soothing and calming teas, waters, and salves. The fresh flowers can be added to facial steams to gently cleanse and treat complexions, keeping them fresh and clear. Chamomile also has gentle bleaching or whitening properties, so it is often featured in nail soaks and hair high-lightening rinses.

To soothe puffy or tired eyes a cool compress made from cold chamomile tea bags, or a cotton cloth soaked in a cold chamomile infusion will do the trick. Simply place the cold compress over your eyes for a few minutes to feel refreshed. Dried or fresh chamomile flowers can be used in creating bath products as a featured ingredient or combined with other dried herbs. Lavender, mint and rose all work well with chamomile when creating relaxing and skin soothing body care products. Here are some recipes featuring this lovely herb for you to try at home.

Note: *To make the Strong Chamomile Tea that is used in the following recipes, use 2 tablespoons of dried chamomile or 2 tea bags to 8 ounces of water.*

Most recipes make a small amount or one time usage but to extend shelf life always store products in a cool, dry, dark spot. If something seems off, it is always better to throw out and mix up a new batch. When using tea or dried herbs it is the same amount of time — when using fresh herbs, you will need to double the amount used, but the time should be the same.

Super Highlighting Hair Rinse

This recipe uses two popular and powerful natural hair highlighting ingredients into one super solution. Chamomile tea brewed fresh from the garden is an old folk recipe for keeping your hair light in color. Lemon juice is what many of us grew up using to add subtle highlights to our hair when outside in the sun. Combined into a hair rinse that can be combed or sprayed on your hair is a natural way to lighten and highlight your hair. This treatment can be drying if used over time so you will want to make sure you condition your hair if needed.

Yield: 8 ounces

1 cup strong chamomile tea
1 tablespoon fresh lemon juice

Mix the ingredients and stir well. Pour into a clean bottle with a tight-fitting lid.

To use, spray or comb through damp hair before going outside. The sun's rays will highlight and lighten your hair over time.

Store in a clean bottle with a tight-fitting lid in a cool, dark spot. For the longest shelf life, you can keep in the refrigerator.

A chamomile tea and lemon juice spritzer can be used to lighten and add highlights to hair. *Janice Cox*

German Chamomile Tea Soother

In Germany, chamomile daisies grow in almost every garden; there is a phrase for this well-loved herb in that country – "alles zutrat," meaning "capable of anything." In fact, around the world chamomile is often referred to as the "physician's plant" because it has so many health applications. This aromatic herb has strong anti-inflammatory and disinfecting qualities and is also soothing to wind-chapped or sunburned skin. This recipe will soothe and calm your complexion and can be made as easily as a cup of tea.

Yield: 8 ounces

2 tablespoons dried chamomile or 2 chamomile tea bags
8 ounces filtered water

In a ceramic or glass container, pour the boiling water over the chamomile and allow it to steep for at least three hours. Strain out the flowers and pour the resulting liquid into a clean container with a tight-fitting lid.

To use, apply to clean skin with a clean cotton pad, or spray on skin; do not rinse off.

Store in clean bottle with a tight-fitting lid in a cool, dark spot. For the longest shelf life, you can keep in the refrigerator.

Chamomile Vinegar Toner

Natural vinegar, such as apple cider or wine vinegar, is often mixed with water and used as a toning spray or splash to help restore the skin's natural pH after cleansing. Most cleansers or soaps are alkaline, so they can alter the skin's natural acid mantle over time. Our skin needs a healthy dose of acid to help keep it clean and protected. Adding chamomile tea, which is healing, soothing, and cleansing for your complexion gives added benefits. If you have sensitive or dry skin double the amount of water called for.

Yield: 4 ounces

1 tablespoon apple cider vinegar, wine vinegar, or chamomile-infused vinegar

1/2 cup strong chamomile tea
1 to 2 tablespoons rosewater or water

Mix all ingredients and pour into a clean container with a tight-fitting lid.

To use, after cleansing, apply to clean skin with a cotton pad. Rinse well with cool water.

Store in clean bottle with a tight-fitting lid in a cool, dark spot. For the longest shelf life, you can keep in the refrigerator which also keeps the toner cool, making it extra refreshing.

Chamomile Tub Tea

Nothing could be easier than creating a bath of your favorite herbal tea blend. I like to envision my bathtub as one giant teapot with myself floating inside. Bathing in the soothing water and sipping a cup of chamomile or my favorite tea blend is a wonderful way to relax and unwind. I simply fill a large tea ball or muslin bag with a combination of dried herbs and hang it under my bath spout, as I fill the tub. If you want an even easier method just tie 4 to 5 tea bags under the waterspout or your shower head. Here are the combinations I like to use:

Yield: 1 to 2 ounces

Stimulating: rosemary, lavender, chamomile, peppermint

Relaxing: chamomile, rose petals, lavender, elderflower

Cleansing: sage, thyme, parsley, chamomile

Refreshing: basil, chamomile, lemon balm, mint

Mix the desired herbs and put them into a tea ball or muslin sack. For a full tub you will need a total of 1/4 cup of dried herbs, or 2 tablespoons for a shower sack. Hang under the waterspout as you run your bath or shower, letting the water flow through it. Gently squeeze your tea bag or allow the tea ball to float in the bath as you bathe. Some people also use the muslin bag as a scrub sack to cleanse and refresh the skin. After bathing discard or compost your herbs.

Easy Chamomile Daisy Soap

White and yellow daisies have always symbolized the ultimate in freshness. Chamomile plants have their own petite flower or daisy that has a fresh, apple-like scent and bright appearance. They also have anti-inflammatory properties, making them well suited for calming sensitive skin. I like to add them to molded soaps. Try placing a fresh flower at the bottom of each mold as a decorative touch. You can use any small container such as a measuring cup, mini loaf pan, or muffin tin as a soap mold.

Yield: 8 ounces, 2 to 3 bars of soap

2 bars grated glycerin soap
1 tablespoon cocoa butter
1 tablespoon water
2 tablespoons dried chamomile flowers or chamomile tea

In a double boiler, place the soap, cocoa butter, and water. Gently heat until the soap and cocoa butter are melted, and you have a thick pudding-like mixture. Stir in the chamomile flowers and spoon the mixture into oiled molds. Let the soap harden, then remove from molds. You may trim your soap using a sharp knife.

Calming Massage Oil

This is an easy infused oil to create and is full of rich oils and relaxing herbs. It would be perfect after the bath or used as a massage oil to soothe tired muscles and calm your mind.

It is important to note when making infused oils that you want to use only dried herbs and flowers. Fresh plant material can introduce moisture into your product that could spoil your oil and cause bacteria to grow.

Ingredients for a relaxing and soothing Chamomile Tub Tea. *Janice Cox*

Yield: 5 ounces

1 tablespoon dried lavender flowers
1 tablespoon dried chamomile daisies
1/2 tablespoon dried scented geranium leaves
1/2 cup grapeseed oil
1 tablespoon apricot kernel oil
2 tablespoons light sesame oil
1/2 teaspoon vitamin E oil

Place the dried herbs inside a clean, dry bottle. Pour the grapeseed, apricot kernel, sesame, and vitamin E oils over them. Cover the opening and shake the contents gently. Let the mixture sit for one to two weeks. Strain through paper coffee filters and store in a clean bottle with a tight-fitting lid.

To use, massage a small amount into your skin. This oil may also be added to your bath or used when making creams or lotion bars.

Chamomile Arrowroot Powder

Arrowroot powder is made from the tropical arrowroot plant. This tall plant has spear-shaped, very shiny green leaves. The fine white starchy powder comes from the dried rhizome found at the plant's base near its roots and is used as a thickener in cosmetic products. It also makes excellent body powder when mixed with dried chamomile. Chamomile is calming and soothing to your skin.

Yield: 4 ounces

1/2 cup arrowroot powder
1 tablespoon finely ground dried chamomile flowers
1 to 2 drops chamomile essential oil

Place the arrowroot powder in a bowl or resealable plastic bag. Add the chamomile flowers and oil and mix well. Pour the scented powder into a clean, dry container.

To use, massage into dry skin or apply with a powder puff after bathing.

Children's Peter Rabbit Bath

We are all familiar with Beatrix Potter's tale of naughty Peter Rabbit who just could not keep out of Mr. MacGregor's Garden. At the end of the tale, Peter's mom gives him a cup of chamomile tea and sends him to bed. She is truly a wise mother, as a good night's rest was just what her little bunny needed. Make up a batch of this chamomile bath for your own little ones.

Yield: 16 ounces

1/2 cup dried chamomile flowers
2 cups oatmeal
1/2 cup cornstarch

Place all the ingredients inside a food processor or blender. Grind until you have a smooth, fine powder. The powder should have the consistency of whole-grain flour. Pour into a clean, airtight container or a resealable plastic bag.

To use, pour 1/2 cup into your bath as you fill the tub, or place inside a muslin tea bag and hang under the flowing water.

Gardener's Hand Cream

Gardening is especially hard on your hands. Dry, rough hands with short nails are usually a good indicator of a beautiful garden. But this does not have to be the case. Massage just a small amount of this rich cream into your hands, making sure to dab some under each nail to condition them and keep out dirt. Always use garden gloves, when possible; this alone will improve the condition of your hands. After cleaning up, use more of this cream to restore any lost moisture and to keep your hands soft and looking their best.

Yield: 4 ounces

3 tablespoons grated beeswax
1/2 tablespoon light oil such as olive, sesame, or sunflower
2 tablespoons strong chamomile tea
1 tablespoon coconut oil

1 teaspoon raw honey
1/8 teaspoon baking soda

Combine all ingredients in a glass ovenproof container or double boiler. Heat in the microwave or over medium heat on the stovetop until all the wax and oils are melted (do not boil), stirring well. Pour the melted mixture into a container or jar and allow to cool completely. Stir again when the mixture has cooled.

To use, massage into hands, feet, and other rough skin spots.

Chamomile for Beauty

Chamomile is an easy-to-grow herb and dries very easily. Make sure you cover it with a cheesecloth or place your plants inside a paper bag with small slits at the top as it dries to keep insects away. I also place my dried herbs in the freezer for 24 hours to make sure nothing is "living" inside the dried plant material. Here are some simple ways to use your dried chamomile:

Chamomile infused oils and natural butters can be used to make skin-soothing creams and lotions. *Janice Cox*

Teas: You can easily make your own chamomile tea or tea blend. Feel free to experiment with blends or try and re-create favorite ones you have enjoyed. One of my favorite combinations is chamomile, lavender, mint and rose.

Infused oils: You can infuse oils and natural butters such as shea, mango and cocoa butter with your dried chamomile. Simply place about a tablespoon of dried plant material in an 8-ounce glass jar of warm oil or natural butter, cover with tight-fitting lid, and let sit for a few weeks in a dark, dry spot. Then reheat and strain your infused oil. You can use this on its own or as a base for lotion bars, creams, and lotions.

After Bath: Keep a spray bottle of chamomile tea in your bathroom and use this mixture as an after-bath splash or spray. The scent is relaxing, and chamomile is healing and soothing to your skin. It is especially calming after shaving. *Store in a cool, dark spot and replace every two weeks.*

Puffy eyes: Cold chamomile-soaked pads or chamomile tea bags placed under your eyes are soothing and refreshing and especially nice after a long day. Chamomile is anti-inflammatory and will help reduce the appearance of puffy under eyes and dark circles.

Hair-lightening: Chamomile has a mild bleaching effect on your hair over time. An effortless way to achieve subtle highlights is to lightly spray your hair with a strong solution of chamomile and water before going outside in the sunshine.

Janice Cox is a garden writer and natural beauty expert. She is the author of *Beautiful Flowers, Beautiful Lavender, Beautiful Luffa, Natural Beauty at Home, Natural Beauty from the Garden, Natural Beauty for All Seasons* and the newly released *Natural Beauty at Home Handbook*. She was the beauty editor for *Herb Quarterly* magazine for more than twenty years and the education chair for The Herb Society of America. She is a member of The International Herb Association. Mrs. Cox loves working with plants and using them in culinary, crafting and wellness projects. Some of her favorite flowers are roses, calendula, lavender, and chamomile.

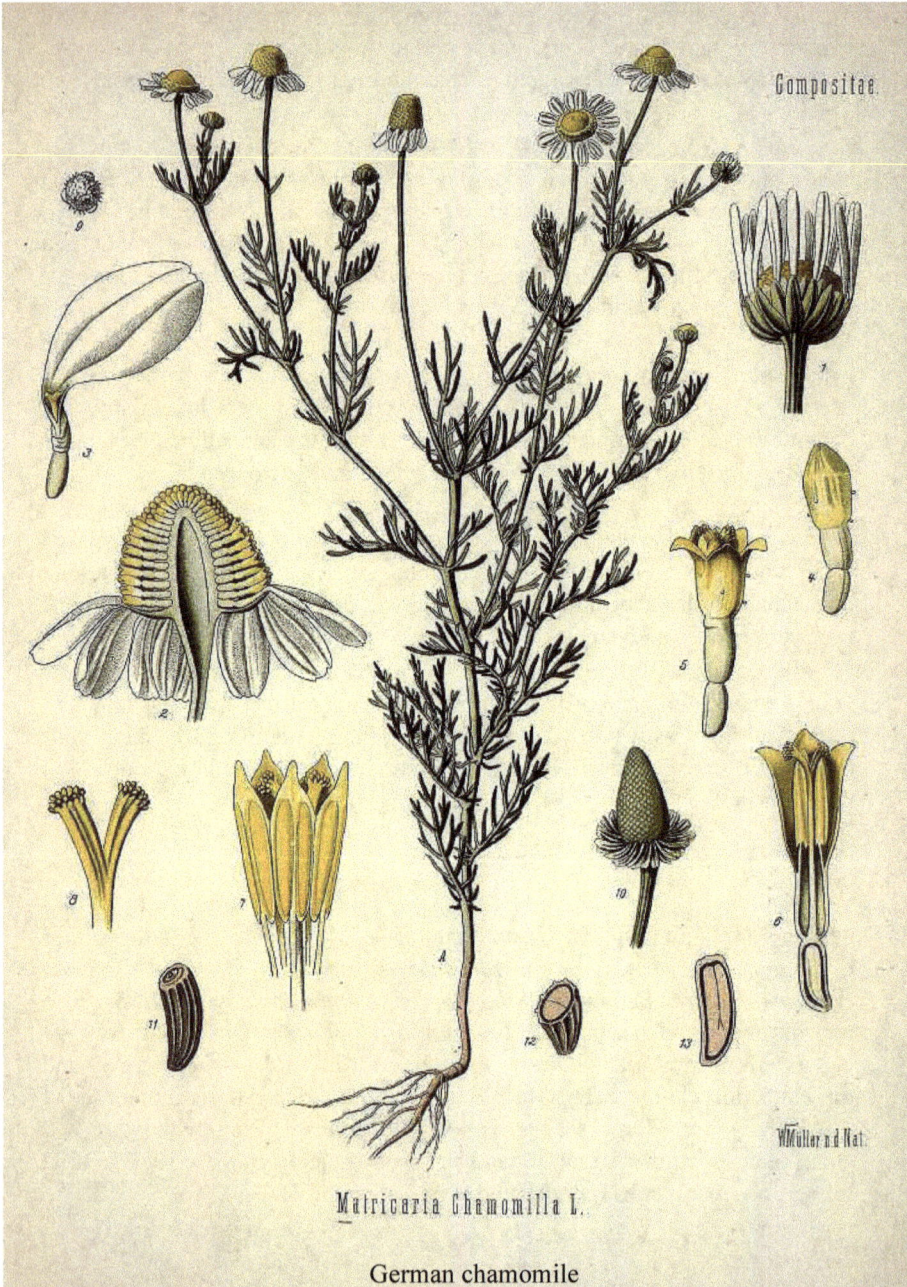

Compositae.

Matricaria Chamomilla L.

German chamomile
Matricaria chamomilla L. Kohler, 1897.

The Medicinal Uses of Chamomile
(*Matricaria chamomilla*)

Daniel Gagnon, Medical Herbalist, RH (AHG)

Chamomile (*Matricaria chamomilla*) [Asteraceae] (Zimmermann 2023)

Synonyms: *Chamomilla recutita, Matricaria recutita, Matricaria suaveolens* (Zimmermann 2023)

Other Common Names

Dutch: Echte kamille, moederkruid (Van Hellemont 1986)

English: German chamomile, Hungarian chamomile (Zimmermann 2023), true chamomile (Wichtl 2004), wild chamomile, chamomilla (Nickell's 1976)

French: Camomille (Valnet 1992), Camomille allemande; Camomille commune, Matricaire (Van Hellemont 1986)

German: Echte kamille (Van Hellemont 1986)

Italian: Camomilla (Bartram 1998)

Russian: Romashka (Hutchens 1973)

Spanish: Manzanilla (Wichtl 2004), Camomile (Bartram 1998)

Unani: Babuna (Aaqil 2021), Babunag, Babunaj (Ghazanfar 1994)

Part Used: The flowers (Hoffmann 1983).

General Description: Chamomile (generally known as German chamomile) is a fragrant annual herb, with flowerheads about 2 cm broad, up to about 1 meter high. It is native to Europe and northern and western Asia. It has naturalized in North America. For commercial purposes, it is extensively cultivated in Russia, Hungary, Romania, Bulgaria, the Czech Republic, Slovakia, Germany, Greece, Brazil Argentina, and Egypt. Frequent changes in interpretation of the scientific name of "German" chamomile have led to great confusion over the past decades (Leung 1996, Srivastava 2010). The current accepted scientific name is *Matricaria chamomilla*, though *Matricaria recutita* and *Chamomilla recutita* are often seen in the scientific literature (Leung 1996).

Herbal Properties: Chamomile possesses a multitude of medicinal properties including analgesic, anodyne (mild), antiallergenic, antibacterial (specifically against *Staphylococcus*), anti-catarrhal, antiemetic, antifungal (specifically against *Candida*), anthelmintic, anti-inflammatory, antimicrobial, anti-peptic ulcer, antiseptic (mild), antispasmodic, bitter, carminative (mild), diaphoretic, emmenagogue, emetic, febrifuge, galactagogue, immunostimulant (mild), nervine, relaxant, sedative (mild), spasmolytic, stimulant, tonic, vulnerary, and wound-healing properties (Bartram 1998, Bone 2003, Duke 1985 and 2002, Hoffmann 1983 & 2003, Menzies-Trull 2003, Nickell 1976, Skenderi 2003).

Constituents: Chamomile flowers contain flavonoids including apigenin, apigetrin, apiin, chryseriol, cosmosiin, hyperoside, lutein, patuletin, quercitin, rutin, and quercimetricin; proazulene compounds including matricin and matricarin; coumarins including umbelliferone, asculetin, chamillin, herniarin, isoscopoletin, and scopoletin; mucilage (3 to 10%) including an inulin-type fructan, a rhamnogalacturonan, and others; a polysaccharide containing D-galacturonic acid as the major constituent; aromatic bitter principles including anthemic acid (up to 3%); choline; anisic-, caffeic-, vanillic-, and syringic acid; amino acids; GABA (gamma-aminobutyric acid); en-in-dicycloether; spiroethers; and others. Chamomile contains variable amounts of volatile oils (0.24 to 1.9%). Chemical races and varieties of the plant as well as the weather and geographical location where the plant is grown affect the amount and composition of the essential oil. Over 120 components have been identified in the oil of chamomile, including the sesquiterpene constituents α-bisabolol (also known as levomenol) bisabolol oxides A, B, and C, farnesene, guaiazulene, and matricin. Chamazulene itself does not occur in the plant but is formed from the sesquiterpene lactone matricin during the steam distillation process to produce the oil. The British Pharmacopoeia recommends that pharmacopoeial-grade dried chamomile flowers should contain no less than 4 mg/kg of the blue essential oil (Bone 2013, Duke 1985 and 2002, Evans 1996, Foster 1993, Leung 1996, Skenderi 2003, Van Hellemont 1986, Wichtl 2004, Wren 1988).

Medicinal Uses:

Internally:

Nervous system For mild to moderate nervous system irritations such as nervous excitability, restlessness, anxiety, generalized anxiety disorder, rheumatic and neuralgic pain. Inability to fall asleep due to restlessness, insomnia, unrefreshing sleep. Highly recommended for night terrors.

Digestive system Calms irritations and spasms of the digestive system and acts as a tonic to the gastrointestinal tract; in minor gastro-inflammatory (indigestion, gastritis), ulcerative (peptic ulcers) and spastic conditions of the gastrointestinal tract. Also useful in bloating, distention, dyspepsia, flatulence, nausea, irritable bowel syndrome, hemorrhoids, travel sickness, nervous diarrhea, etc. Used frequently for mucositis, specifically inflammation of the oral cavity and esophagus of neck and throat cancer patients.

Reproductive system It is used in primary dysmenorrhea (painful menstruation) where there is no overt pathology. Also useful in premenstrual tension, amenorrhea, menorrhagia, leucorrhea, and mastitis.

Respiratory system Helpful as an inhalation for inflammation of the upper respiratory tract; build-up of mucous in the nose, ears and eyes.

Skin Useful against a variety of skin conditions such as eczema, impetigo (e.g., *Staph* skin infection), psoriasis, urticaria, wound dermabrasion, leg ulceration, diaper rash, or as it is known in England, nappy rash, insect bites, sunburn, radiation burns from cancer treatment (in conjunction with *Aloe vera*). It stimulates wound healing and prevents secondary bacterial infections.

Children Especially useful in children, as it is effective against a myriad of conditions and, yet, is relatively mild tasting. Use chamomile with babies and young children who experience tummy aches or colic, are hyperactive, irritable, or cranky, or when they can't settle down and/or fall asleep.

Miscellaneous Useful in the early stages of fever, measles (warm tea), pin and thread worm.

Antimicrobial The essential oil has substantial bactericidal and fungicidal activities, against Gram-positive bacteria (e.g., *Staphylococcus aureus*),

Dried chamomile flowers are easily crushed and ground in a mortar and pestle. *Susan Belsinger*

Gram negative bacteria (e.g., and the fungus *Candida albicans* (Bartram 1998, Leung 1996, Menzies-Trull 2003, Skenderi 2003, Bone 2013).

Externally:

For inflammation of the mouth (aphthous stomatitis) and throat, use as a mouthwash, gargle, paint, or gel; in otitis media, use as eardrops; for red bump on eyelid (known as chalazion). For sore nipples, hemorrhoids, and varicose veins, use a wet compress or poultice. For anal or genital (e.g., vaginal) inflammations, use as a sitz bath. It has been and continues to be used as an ingredient in numerous hair wash, hair dye, and skin care products (Skenderi 2003). It is said to lighten hair color (Menzies-Trull 2003, Paris 1971) or add luster to blond hair (Uphof 1968). In cases of conjunctivitis, use a cold tea, filter the tea well before using. Use it as an eyewash, although, in a few individuals, it may cause an allergic reaction (Bone 2003). In skin issues, use as a poultice with a few drops of myrrh (*Commiphora myrrha*) extract (Bartram 1998).

Introduction to the Medicinal Uses of Chamomile

Chamomile has been known and used as an herbal medicine for a very, very long time. Recently, paleontologists studied the calculus on the teeth of 5 Neanderthal remains found at the El Sidrón Caves in the Asturias region of Northern Spain. These remains dated from approximately 24,000 to 30,000 years ago (Hardy 2012). In the dental calculus of these individuals, the researchers identified compounds from two plants, chamomile and yarrow (*Achillea millefolium*). These tooth scrapings suggest that Neanderthals chewed on medicinal plants to soothe their upsets. The researchers believe that these two plants' medicinal activities were known and that the selection of these two herbs were probably deliberate (Hardy 2013).

Relatively more recently, around 2,000 years ago, the Egyptians, Greeks, and Romans administered chamomile as a fever-reducing remedy, as an emmenagogue to promote menstruation, as well as medicine against liver diseases and intestinal pains (Paris 1971). The Greek physician Dioscorides and the Roman naturalist Pliny recommended chamomile to treat headaches and kidney, liver, and bladder problems. In India, ancient Ayurvedic physicians used the flowers for similar indications (Castleman 1991). Seventeenth century English herbalist Nicholas Culpepper recommended chamomile for fevers, digestive problems, aches, pains, jaundice, kidney stones, "dropsy" (congestive heart failure) and "to bring down women's courses" (promote menstruation) (Culpepper 1814). Tyler (1993) writes that the Germans describe it as *alles zutraut*, "capable of anything." They also refer to *Matricaria recutita* as the "genuine chamomile." He points out that chamomile flowers are currently registered as an approved herbal medicine in many European pharmacopeia (Paris 1971).

Homeopathic Description of *Chamomilla* remedy

Over the years, I have found that homeopathy describes the symptom picture of a remedy in a way that is very useful to target the exact remedy and indications for an individual's needs. Investigating chamomile's homeopathic indications helped me get a better understanding and feeling for the herb itself.

Clarke's (1982) signature symptom for *Chamomilla* is: an individual who suddenly manifests "spiteful, sudden, and uncivil irritability." This indication is especially true when applied to children. Tyler (1952) writes that a fitting description of the chamomile personality is "Cannot bear it." He suggests that the person who best benefits from this remedy usually can't bear himself/ herself, can't bear others, and can't bear pain. The individual can't bear things either: first, he wants whatever object, then, when given to him, he hurls it away. Everything seems simply intolerable. A sick baby will whine, and howl, and insist on being carried. The moment the tired mother or father tries to sit down or to lay the baby down in the crib, the whining and howling start afresh. Another key indication for *Chamomilla* is that the symptoms are worse at night (Tyler 1952). In my experience, the child or person who experiences these symptoms not only benefits from taking this homeopathic remedy, but also benefits from drinking the herb as a tea.

The Medicinal Uses of Chamomile

Nervous system Chamomile is without a doubt one of the best known and most used relaxing nervine herbs in North America and Europe. Although it is not the strongest nervine herb, chamomile is safe and effective in most types of anxiety, including generalized anxiety disorder, depression, and other stress-related conditions (Viola 1995, Amsterdam 2009, 2012, and 2019, Saadatmand 2024). It soothes the nervous system and calms the agitated person. It is especially useful when anxiety or stress aggravates digestive issues such as loss of appetite, nausea, heartburn, acid reflux, colic, gas, bloating, nervous diarrhea, or nervous dyspepsia (Grieves 1982, Bone 2003). When stress levels in a person's life are unrelenting, the severity of digestive disturbances tends to progress and leads to ulceration of the gastric or intestinal tissues (Szelenyi 1979).

Chamomile flowers are rich in essential oil containing chamazulene and α-bisabolol, two constituents that have been shown in clinical trials to soothe, heal, and repair damaged mucous membranes (Al-Hashem 2010). Not only does chamomile ease physical symptoms but it also reduces psychological tension and strain. Chamomile has been shown to work on the peripheral nervous system, thus relaxing the whole body (Bone 2013).

In Ayurvedic medicine, chamomile is considered a *sattvic* herb, an herb that creates a balanced, harmonious and/or serene mind and attitude. In moderate amounts, chamomile is said to be good for all ayurvedic constitutions. It is reputed to balance emotions and serves as a harmonizing addition to herbal formulas. It calms the nervous system and can be used as poultice to calm nerve pains. Additionally, the herb is considered especially useful for *pitta* constitutions. Individuals with a *pitta* constitution tend to suffer from acidic stomach, heartburn, oversensitive skin, and extreme body heat (Frawley 2001).

In France, chamomile is often recommended to treat facial neuralgia and migraine headaches. Facial neuralgia is a chronic pain condition that causes sudden, severe facial pain. This condition is also known as *tic douloureux* or trigeminal neuralgia and is often experienced as sharp and shooting pains in the jaw, teeth, and/or gums (Valnet 1992, Mésségué 1975). Henri Leclerc (1976), a medical doctor who chose to practice herbal medicine for many decades, turned to chamomile for patients who suffered from migraines resistant to "classic" pharmaceutical products. He reports that many sufferers were relieved with intensive concentrated chamomile tea. In some cases, he prescribed ingestion of 2 to 4 grams of freshly ground chamomile flowers (Leclerc 1976). Recent clinical trials have shown that the herb, applied topically, delivers relief for migraine sufferers (Zagaran 2014 and 2018). Chamomile demonstrated significant analgesic and neuropathic pain-relieving effects. Both water and alcohol extracts were shown to decrease the cancer drug cisplatin-induced pain and inflammation even better than morphine (Abbas Abad 2011).

Conventional drug treatments for Generalized Anxiety Disorder (GAD) come with substantial side effects, dependence, and/or withdrawal syndrome. Many individuals suffering from GAD seek complementary and alternative medicine (CAM) therapies for their symptoms rather than conventional therapy. In 2009, chamomile was the subject of a clinical trial for moderate generalized anxiety disorder. Researchers concluded that chamomile has anxiolytic activity in patients with mild to moderate generalized anxiety disorders. Additionally, side effects, dependence, and/or withdrawal syndromes were negligeable (Amsterdam 2009). Three years later, in a follow-up study, the same researchers confirmed the positive results when treating generalized anxiety disorders with chamomile. In this clinical trial, some of the subjects chosen for inclusion in the study were suffering from GAD as well as depression (Amsterdam 2012). In 2016, another clinical trial was conducted and, once again, chamomile produced a clinically meaningful reduction in GAD symptoms over 8 weeks. The response rate in the chamomile group was comparable to those observed during conventional anxiolytic drug therapy. Adverse events were negligible (Mao 2014). In 2019, Amsterdam and associates analyzed the two studies that extended to GAD patients who were also suffering from depression and concluded that the healing seemed more effective when the patients were suffering from both GAD and depression (Amsterdam 2019). Additionally, in all three studies, the patients with favorable expectations about the chamomile treatment did better than those without such expectations; and they experienced fewer side effects (Keefe 2016).

Chamomile is very rich in *apigenin*, a flavonoid found in plant-derived foods. In scientific studies, apigenin has demonstrated excellent nerve protective properties (Moshfegh 2017). For example, this constituent has been reported to exert a neuroprotective effect against oxidative stress in neurological disorders, such as cerebral ischemia, a type of stroke (Chandrashekarh 2010). In a recent laboratory experiment, Kim and colleagues (2019) demonstrated that apigenin has a significant neuroprotective effect against peripheral nerve degeneration. This research found that apigenin protects human beings against nerve degeneration in four ways. First, it prevents the degradation of axons, the long fibers of nerve cells that transmit information between neurons. Second, apigenin prevents myelin degeneration, thus limiting the damage or destruction of the nerve cell covering. Third, it prevents trans-dedifferentiation, the regression of neurons that leads to loss of nerve function. Fourth, apigenin assists in the proliferation of Schwann cells, which are specialized cells that play essential roles in the development, maintenance, function, and regeneration of peripheral nerves. Apigenin speeds up the regeneration of nerve cells after they suffer damage. This study demonstrated that apigenin might be an excellent nutrient to treat peripheral neurodegenerative diseases (Kim 2019). Other rich apigenin-containing herbs include parsley, spinach, and celery seeds (Mushtaq 2023). Assuming you are not doing so currently, consider adding these four herbs to your diet regularly. It's interesting to consider how science always circles back to green leafy vegetables and other herbal allies to help us meet our needs for both well-known and lesser-known nutrients.

Sleep Chamomile has facilitated sleep for hundreds of years. It assists and allows tightly-wound individuals to unwind, those who are stressed to relax, and anxious people to feel more tranquil. A mild tea acts as a gentle sleep aid, especially in children (Foster 1993). According to Mrs. Grieve, chamomile is considered a preventive and the "sole" sure-fire remedy for nightmares (Grieve 1982). Many scientists believe that apigenin is chamomile's main constituent that has a positive effect on sleep. This flavonoid acts by binding to benzodiazepine receptors found in the brain, reducing anxiety and exerting slight sedative effects (Viola 1995). However, it's my opinion that the jury is still out on that matter. I am still convinced it is ALL of chamomile's constituents that deliver good sleep results. Some constituents help relax the person, others comfort the digestive system, while still others soothe anxiety and reduce stress levels. It takes all of them to generate a deep, sound, and regenerative sleep.

Digestive Aid Maurice Mésségué (1975), a renowned French herbalist, writes that his grandmother, a practicing herbalist, gave him infusions of chamomile whenever she thought he might have intestinal worms. Mésségué's father, also a practicing herbalist, recommended the herb either as a strong tea taken internally or as a tea-soaked compress or liniment used on the abdomen of individuals suffering from stomach troubles, cramps, colic, and intestinal spasms. He noted that a cup of hot chamomile tea is a simple and effective way to relieve indigestion. Not only is the tea used to promote the proper digestive system function, but it has also been shown to soothe stomach or intestinal inflammation in gastritis and prevent ulceration of these digestive tissues (Hoffmann 2003). In England, the tea is taken one hour or more before a main meal to increase the appetite and digestive functions of aged individuals (Grieve 1982). An infusion of the flower heads from a close relative of chamomile, *Matricaria aurea*, growing wild in Saudi Arabia, is made into a tea for colic, cramps and stomach aches (Ghazanfar 1994),

Chamomile has been shown to possess substantial antiulcer activity in vitro. Animal studies have shown that it reduces the occurrence of ulceration induced by stress, alcohol, and NSAIDS (indomethacin, ibuprofen, and aspirin). More so, used during high stress situations, chamomile has demonstrated ulcer-protective activity (Petronilho 2012). A laboratory study found that chamomile extract was as effective as the drug sulfasalazine in reducing the production of inflammatory compounds after inflammatory

stimulus. The researchers concluded that the observed modulatory effects support the use of chamomile supplementation as a promising tool for the prevention and management of ulcerative colitis (Menghini 2016). In a clinical trial, chamomile extract was the most potent herb to decrease gastric acidity and acid input. Additionally, it significantly increased the production of gastric mucin, a substance produced by our stomach that acts as a protectant to the digestive membranes of the stomach and intestines (Abbas Abad 2011). Mucins coat the surface of the stomach and the intestines, protect the gastrointestinal tract and are important to prevent *H. pylori* colonization, the principal cause of gastric or duodenal inflammation and/or ulceration. (Byrd 2000). Another research group discovered that chamomile caused the largest increase of gastric mucin content, as compared to 10 other herbs tested, including licorice (*Glycyrrhiza glabra*) (Khayyal 2011).

As Rudolph Weiss (1988) reports, chamomile does not merely give symptomatic relief in stomach and intestinal ulcerations, it actually heals the injured mucous membranes. Weiss emphasizes that it is necessary to give chamomile in sufficient quantity and for a time period long enough for the ulceration to heal thoroughly. He states that a single cup of tea during the day is far from being adequate to heal the damaged tissues. He prescribes one cup during the course of the morning, preferably one hour before lunch, another cup around 5 pm or about one before dinner, and lastly, one cup before going to bed. He reports that this frequency has given him excellent results. If a stomach ulcer is especially painful, he prescribes a strong cup of chamomile tea first thing in the morning, while still in bed. After drinking the cup of strong tea, the person lies on their back for 5 to 10 minutes, then turns on the left side, for the same amount of time, then on the right side for 5 to 10 minutes, and finally laying on the stomach for another 5 to 10 minutes (Weiss 1988). Significant relief is usually experienced within a week.

A person experiencing gastrointestinal tract ulceration should consider adding chamomile to the diet. Additionally, chamomile is a must-use herb when a person needs to take any drugs that are known to have ulcerogenic activity on the gastrointestinal tract, as it provides a substantial layer of protection (Jabri 2017).

A common complication of patients who receive head and neck radiation and chemotherapy treatments is mucositis. In this medical scenario, mucositis manifests as an inflammation of the mucous membranes that line the oral cavity, specifically the mouth (stomatitis), and the esophagus. Chamomile extract has been used in clinical studies either prior to or right after the radiation and/or chemotherapy treatments. Researchers reported a rapid resolution of the oral and esophageal inflammation. Furthermore, patients reported that chamomile extract provided them with an analgesic effect, allowing them to eat solid foods more easily and comfortably than without herbal treatment (Shabanloei 2009, Braga 2015). The researchers also reported that the affected mucosal tissues were able to regenerate more quickly with the help of chamomile than with placebos (Carl 1991, Mazokopakis 2005, Tadbir 2015, Dos Reis 2016, Gomes 2018, and Elhadad 2020). Additionally, because of its analgesic effects, chamomile provided a better quality of life to individuals who suffered from mouth ulceration (Ramos-e-Silva 2006), especially if the ulcers were of the recurrent aphthous stomatitis type (Seyyedi 2014).

Chamomile regulates peristalsis, the movement of food through the digestive system, and because of this regulating action on the digestive system, can treat both diarrhea and constipation (McIntyre 1994). It is well known for soothing spasms, colic, abdominal pain, gastroenteritis, wind and distention, particularly when these symptoms are aggravated by stress and tension. The volatile oils present in the flower have been shown to prevent and/or speed up the healing of ulcers when used internally or externally. Thus, it is an excellent remedy for gastritis, peptic or duodenal ulcers, as well as leg ulcers. It is known that peptic ulcers often go hand in hand with chronic constipation. When the use of flax (*Linum usitatissimum*) seeds and/or psyllium (*Plantago psyllium*) husks do not resolve the constipation, the addition of senna (*Cassia acutifolia*) leaves are beneficial and can be used with chamomile (Weiss 1988). Adding caraway (*Carum carvi*) seeds to this tea reduces or prevents intestinal griping that can occur with the use of senna leaves.

Herbal practitioners have recommended the use of chamomile for anal and genital issues, either as compresses or sitz baths (Schaffner 1992).

Anti-inflammatory Properties Chamomile has been shown to inhibit the formation of inflammatory compounds in the body. Science has revealed that more than one constituent of the flower contributes to this soothing action. For example, one of chamomile's constituents is called *chamazulene*. Chamazulene has been shown to inhibit the activation of an inflammatory compound called leukotriene B4. Leukotrienes are pro-inflammatory substances that recruit and activate white blood cells called neutrophils, monocytes, and eosinophils, which create tissue inflammation. Leukotriene B4 stimulates the production of proinflammatory cytokines and mediators, which can start and prolong inflammation. Leukotrienes can activate and fan the fires of cystic fibrosis, inflammatory bowel disease, psoriasis, and asthma. In other words, leukotrienes are known to start and keep inflammation going in these tissues. Chamazulene is an excellent fire extinguisher to snuff out these inflammatory compounds. It quells the inflammation and returns the tissues to a normal state (Safayhi 1994). Chamazulene is only one of many other chamomile compounds that have been found to possess excellent anti-inflammatory properties (Srivastava 2009). Additionally, it has been shown that both water AND alcohol soluble constituents have active anti-inflammatory properties (Bone 2013).

Women's Health Chamomile has been a woman's friend for centuries. Its Latin name, *Matricaria,* is derived from the word *matrix,* meaning womb, reflecting the many benefits that this herb has on the female reproductive system (Stansbury 2018). It is an excellent antispasmodic against menstrual cramps. Consider combining it with Cramp Bark (*Viburnum opulus*) bark and Wild Yam (*Dioscorea villosa*) root to achieve even better uterine antispasmodic results. It is specifically indicated for PMS symptoms such as anxiety and irritability that can be accompanied by diarrhea and intestinal upset (Stanberry 2018). Chamomile has literally been used for hundreds of years to promote the menstrual flow in delayed menstruation or simple amenorrhea (lack of menstruation), especially when due to stress (Hutchens 1973). It also relaxes uterine spasms and relieves painful periods. It is used to reduce menopausal symptoms, and to relieve mastitis, premenstrual headaches and migraines (McIntyre 1994).

Chamomile, called *manzanilla* in Spanish, is perhaps the most popular Mexican and Mexican-American herb. It helps relieve nausea and sickness in pregnancy. In Mexico, when a woman experiences painful labor, her midwife will often prepare a pot of *té de manzanilla.* If the pregnant woman is having false labor, chamomile tea calms and stops the contractions. However, the same tea makes the contractions more efficient and more rhythmic when it is true labor; thus the pregnant woman and her midwife know that she is transitioning toward delivery (Kay 1996). Chamomile relaxes the tension felt during delivery and lessens the pain of contractions (McIntyre 1994).

For women who experience menorrhagia (defined as menstrual bleeding that is heavier than normal and/or lasts longer than 7 days), chamomile is an excellent addition to a formula to treat this condition. Chamomile enhances the regulation and balancing of the menstrual cycle. A woman might also consider adding cinnamon (*Cinnamomum verum*) bark to the formulation since it has been shown to decrease excessive bleeding (Jaafarpour 2015).

Chamomile is a simple, classic uterine tonic herb and a very valuable herb to treat dysmenorrhea, especially spastic dysmenorrhea (Holmes 1989). Women suffering from uterine, intestinal, and pelvic cramps should promptly sip on a cup of strong chamomile tea at the first sign of cramping (Weiss 1988). Recent clinical trials showed moderate pain-relieving effects in women who were suffering from painful menstruation (dysmenorrhea) (Shabani 2022). It is especially helpful when painful menstruations are accompanied by diarrhea, bloating, gas, irritability and anxiety (Romm 2010). The authors of a systematic review of the clinical studies done on this herb concluded that chamomile is an effective treatment for primary dysmenorrhea and for reducing excessive menstrual bleeding (Niazi 2021).

Chamomile can be used as a cream or a tea-soaked compress to treat cracked sore nipples (Mabey 1988). It can also be used as a douche for vaginal infections. Chamomile is also highly antiseptic and is effective against thrush, often caused by *Candida albicans* (McIntyre 1994). Sitting in a bowl of chamomile tea is wonderfully soothing for cystitis and hemorrhoids (McIntyre 1994).

Children's Health Chamomile is the herb of choice for children when it's bedtime and they are still wound up from the day's activities. Reach for this herb when they are anxious or irritable from teething. During dentition, children may experience earaches, neuralgic pains, as well as stomach disorders. Make a strong infusion of the flowers (1/2 ounce for one quart of water), add to the bathwater, and let them soak in it for a few minutes. Their sensitive skin quickly absorbs chamomile's active constituents. The flowers calm and soothe their nervous system. Chamomile is also an effective late-night tea to help ensure a restful sleep (Grieve 1982).

Chamomile can be used as a traditional remedy in children's simple acute diarrhea. Double blind clinical trials with young children between the ages of 6 months and 6 years showed that apple pectin (from apple sauce), chamomile extract, and simple rehydration fluids restored normal bowel function much quicker than placebo treatment (De La Motte 1997, Becker 2011).

To make 1 liter of Oral Rehydration Salts (ORS) solution, follow these four simple steps:

[To increase the effectiveness of this rehydration solution, substitute one liter of chamomile infusion for the liter of water. Use 5 scant tablespoons of chamomile flowers in one liter of hot water, let sit for 15 minutes covered; filter, and use this infused chamomile tea instead of the liter of water.]

1. Measure 1 liter (33 liquid ounces) of water - 5 cups (each cup about 200 ml.).

2. Add six level teaspoons of sugar to the water.

3. Add 1/2 level teaspoon of salt to the water.

4. Stir the mixture until the sugar and salt are completely dissolved.

The dosage for children under the age of 2 is 1/2 cupful (4 ounces) of ORS after each watery stool; for children above the age of 2 at least one cupful (8 ounces) of ORS after each watery stool. For adults, drink frequent sips of ORS every 5 minutes until urination becomes normal. It is normal to urinate 4 to 5 times a day. Note that this rehydration fluid will not increase the diarrhea. The chamomile-enhanced ORS solution can be used anytime a child or adult has diarrhea, is vomiting, has a fever, or is dehydrated from excessive sweating.

Skin, Wound Healing, Inflammation, and Itching The topical application of chamomile as a strong tea, cream, or compress has been found to be effective in accelerating the healing of burns, sores, abscesses, radiation-induced dermatitis, acute weeping skin disorders, decubitus ulcers (aka bedsores), fistulae, scalds, incisions, wounds, hemorrhoids, mastitis, leukorrhea, and leg ulcers (Schulz 2004, Jarrahi 2008 and 2010). A standardized chamomile cream was compared with steroidal and non-steroidal skin preparations in the treatment of eczema. The chamomile cream showed a similar effectiveness to a hydrocortisone cream and was superior to another nonsteroidal anti-inflammatory agent (bufexamac). Chamomile cream was also shown to be more effective than a glucocorticoid preparation (fluocortin butyl ester) (Bone 2013).

In a double-blind trial, the therapeutic efficacy of chamomile extract was tested on 14 patients. To evaluate the effectiveness of the extract, the researchers examined the epithelial and drying effect on a weeping wound area after dermabrasion of tattoos. They concluded that the healing and drying process was faster than the placebo treatment. The investigators noted a significant decrease of the weeping wound area, as well as an increase in the drying process of the wound with chamomile extract (Glowania 1987).

Respiratory Health The health benefits of chamomile also are applicable to the respiratory system. The steam inhalation of chamomile's essential oil delivers its valuable constituents to the inflamed mucous membranes of the sinuses and lung tissues (Schaffner 1992). Add to that chamomile's mild antimicrobial properties, which ensure that the respiratory tract stays free of harmful microorganisms. Its anti-catarrhal (anti-mucus) properties stimulate the elimination of excess mucus from the sinuses, lungs, and digestive system. Chamomile is useful in treating head colds, mild lung congestion, allergies, and hay fever (Hoffmann 2003). Steam inhalations help relieve asthma, hay fever, catarrh and sinusitis. The tea helps to bring down a fever. It can also be given for colds, flu, sore throat, and coughs (McIntyre 1994).

Allergies Allergies can manifest in many ways, including seasonal rhinitis, sinusitis, hay fever, eczema (internally and externally), asthma, and food allergies. Mast cells are located throughout the body, release histamine and other inflammatory substances when provoked, and cause local or systemic allergic reactions when challenged by pollen or other allergenic substances. In an in vitro study, Chandrashekhar (2011) and his colleagues demonstrated the antiallergic activity of chamomile. The researchers concluded that chamomile stabilizes mast cells.

Fevers For centuries, chamomile has been used to reduce all types of fevers. Before the discovery of cinchona bark (*Cinchona officinalis*) in the 1600s, chamomile was the go-to plant for intermittent fevers and as an effective remedy for malarial fevers. Egyptians, Greeks and Romans used it as a reliable febrifuge, a remedy that reduces fevers (Paris 1971). Dioscorides, a Greek physician, pharmacologist, botanist, author of *Materia Medica* who lived from 40 to 90 AD, recommended powdered chamomile flowers to take away fever bouts (a.k.a. intermittent fevers). In their book *Traité de thérapeutique et de matière médicale,* Trousseau and Pidoux (1877) state that many early authors, including Dioscorides, praised the properties of chamomile as a febrifuge, and always recommended powdered flowers as the most effective preparation for fevers at the dose of 2 to 4 grams. Most early authors also suggested that chamomile powder is best used in combination with other astringent herbs, such as blackberry or raspberry leaves, to prevent excessive looseness of the bowels from the chamomile flower powder.

A simple infusion is the easiest way to enjoy the benefits of chamomile.
Susan Belsinger

Grading chamomile flowers and oil

Flowers Before World War II, chamomile herb was often graded into six categories. Type 1 grade, also called "Extra," was literally hand-picked flowers, didn't contain any stems, was of beautiful appearance, and commanded three times the price of the other grades. Types II, III, and IV were picked with a special comb designed specifically for harvesting the flowers. The three grades were distinguished by increasing amounts of stem material and foreign matters (e.g., clinging bits of weed or grass) in it. Type V, also called "bath chamomile," consisted wholly of flowers with attached stems and was the quality used for external applications. Finally, type VI, also called "chamomile dust" consisted of sifted out dust. Note that it takes approximately five kilograms of freshly-picked flowers to yield 1 kilogram of air-dried flowers (Guenther 1952). Not much has changed since then. However, the "Extra" grade rarely makes it to the marketplace, except when purchased directly from a farmer/herbalist. Because of the amount of time it takes to harvest chamomile flowers by hand, the price will also be proportionally higher.

Oil High-grade chamomile flowers are too expensive to be used for essential oil production. For distillation purposes, grades IV, V, and VI are usually employed. When chamomile oil is freshly distilled, it is of a deep, intense, blue color with a characteristic odor and bitter aromatic taste. Chamazulene, present between 1 to 15% in freshly distilled oil, is one of the main contributors to the color. However, under the influence of light, air, and time, the oil degrades. The deep blue color of the oil gradually changes to green and then to brown. The yield of oil from the flowers is from about 0.10% to approximately 0.50%. Thus, it takes between 200 to 1,000 pounds of flowers to produce 1 pound of oil (Guenther 1952). That's why authentic chamomile oil is so expensive. Farmers have noted that the presence of weeds at critical stages of plant development can reduce chamomile essential oil yield by 30 to 40% (Wikifarmer 2024).

How to Use Chamomile as Medicine

As with many essential oil-containing herbs, it is best to use the fresh herb to make medicinal products such as tinctures or ointments. When using dried flowers, they should look fairly intact and have a strong aromatic scent.

Internally Make tea from the dried flowers; 1 scant tablespoon for each cup of just-boiling water. Infuse 10 to 20 minutes, covered. The tea should always be prepared in a covered vessel as it prevents the escape of active constituents. Use one cupful freely, up to 4 times a day (Grieve 1982, Bartram 1998). Another way to prepare the infusion is to let 1/2 to 1 ounce of the flowers infuse in one pint of just-boiling water, covered. Infuse 10 to 20 minutes, and filter. Use in doses of one tablespoon to one wineglass (about 5 ounces) three or four times a day (Grieve 1982).

Make fresh chamomile flower herbal extract/tincture (1 part herb to 4 parts 45% to 55% alcohol). Take 15 to 60 drops two to four times a day (morning, noon, afternoon, and night) (Bartram 1998). Studies have shown that alcohol extracts made from the fresh herb have more active constituents than extracts made with dried flowers. Second best is the use of carefully harvested and shade-dried flowers to make the medicines for health purposes (Bone 2013).

Externally For an infusion, steep two teaspoons of flowers per cup of hot water, covered, for 10 minutes. Filter. Use as a wash for skin diseases and inflammation of all types including acne and hemorrhoids (Valnet 1992). For a compress, fill a small muslin or linen bag with 1/2 to 1 ounce of the flowers, immerse in 1/2 pint of just-boiling water, wring out excess liquid, and apply the bag over swellings, neuralgias, and inflammatory pain of any affected area. This has proved invaluable in relieving swelling of the face caused by abscesses (Grieve 1982). Repeatedly moisten the bag when dry and reapply (Grieve 1982, Bartram 1998).

Chamomile baths can be prepared to lessen pain and inflammation. Use a handful of the dried flowers in 1 pint (500 ml) of just-boiling water, let it infuse for 15 minutes covered, strain to remove the herb, and add the strained liquid to the sitz bath or the bath water (Bartram 1998).

Safety There are no safety concerns surrounding the use of this herb. The *Botanical Safety Handbook* classifies chamomile as a **Safety Class 1** herb, an herb that can be safely consumed when used appropriately (Gardner 2013).

Pregnancy and Lactation The authors of *Botanical Safety Handbook* note that while their review did not identify any concerns for use of chamomile during pregnancy or while nursing, safety has not been conclusively established (Gardner 2013). However, in England, herbalists do not hesitate to recommend and prescribe chamomile during pregnancy or while breast-feeding (Bartram 1998). We are discussing German chamomile here, *Matricaria chamomilla*, in the form of tea, extract, or capsule; and not Roman chamomile, *Chamaemelum nobile*.

Contraindications None known (Gardner 2013).

Adverse Effects and Side Effects In large doses, chamomile has been known to cause vomiting (Bartram 1998). In Ayurvedic medicine, individuals with a *vata* constitution tend to suffer from dry skin, constipation, brittle hair, nails, or bones, as well as rigidity of the mind and/or body. It is said that very large quantities of chamomile may aggravate *Vata* constitutions and may cause vomiting. To prevent this potential issue, adding a little ginger (*Zingiber officinale*) to the chamomile helps make it a balanced beverage and counters any emetic effect that chamomile might possess (Frawley 2001).

In Germany, the health authorities (German Standard License) require the following label warning on chamomile products: The infusion should not be used near the eyes (Gardner 2013).

In very rare cases, there have been confirmed reports of contact allergies to chamomile and other Asteraceae plants (arnica, echinacea, feverfew, ragweed, tansy, yarrow) in hypersensitive individuals (Gardner 2013). Scientists believe that chamomile's contact allergy is caused by a constituent found in the plant called sesquiterpene lactone (Skenderi 2003).

In 1984, a group of researchers compiled every chamomile-induced allergic reaction that was reported in worldwide medical literature from 1887 to 1982. They did not find any death reports and only found a total of 50 reactions. Of those, 45 cases were attributed to Roman chamomile (*Chamaemelum nobile,* formerly known as *Anthemis nobilis)* and only 5 from German chamomile (*Matricaria recutita*), this last one being the herb most often used in the United States (Tyler 1993). The relative infrequency of chamomile hypersensitivity should not deter normal persons from consuming it. Obviously, should you experience an allergic reaction to it, stop using it.

Drug Interactions The *Botanical Safety Handbook* has classified chamomile as "an herb for which no clinically relevant interactions are expected" (Gardner 2013).

Pharmacological Considerations Some scientists have suggested that chamomile may be an herb with the "theoretical potential" for interacting with warfarin (an anticoagulant drug) due to the coumarin content of the herb. However, it's important to note that the coumarin content of chamomile consists of the coumarin derivatives herniarin and umbelliferone. In the case of herniarin, this constituent has been shown to possess slight hemostatic (blood coagulating) activity (Ahmad 1997). As for umbelliferone, no evidence of anticoagulant activity has been shown (Egan 1990, Feuer 1974, Pelkonen 1997). Therefore, the "theoretical potential" for chamomile to interact with warfarin is highly improbable. In other words, it's a very safe herb when using an anticoagulant drug

Other Plant Allies Use with valerian (*Valeriana officinalis*) root, passion-flower (*Passiflora incarnata*) herb, and hops (*Humulus lupulus*) strobiles, equal parts, for nervous excitability. Use 1 part of licorice (*Glycyrrhiza glabra*) root and 4 parts of chamomile flower for gastric ulcers and chronic dyspepsia. Chamomile flower also works well with peppermint (*Mentha piperita*) leaf and lemon balm (*Melissa officinalis*) herb for digestive issues (Bartram 1998). Use with poke (*Phytolacca decandra*) root for mastitis (Menzies-Trull 2003).

Other Uses Chamomile has been used for flavoring fine French-type liqueurs. It is used in perfumery and for scenting chamomile shampoos. It is also used in Europe for flavoring tobacco. Chamomile oil has been used as a solvent of platinum chloride in the process of coating glass and porcelain with platinum (Uphof 1968).

References

Azeem M. Aaqil, AM., Mahboob, S., and Nafees, KM. 2021. "Phytochemical and pharmacological studies and evidence-based indications of Babuna (*Matricaria chamomilla* L.): A Review." *Ayushdhara*. 8(6): 3700-3708.

Abbas Adad, AN., Kayate Nouri, MH., Gharjanie, A., and Tavakoli, F. 2011. "Effect of *Matricaria chamomilla* Hydroalcoholic Extract on Cisplatin-induced Neuropathy in Mice." *Chinese Journal of Natural Medicines*. 9(2): 126–131.

Ahmad, A., and Misra, L. 1997. "Isolation of herniarin and other constituents from *Matricaria chamomila* flowers." *Int. J. Pharmacog*. 35(2): 121-125.

Al-Hashem, FH. 2010. "Gastroprotective effects of aqueous extract of Chamomilla recutita against ethanol-induced gastric ulcers." *Saudi Med J*. 31(11): 1211-1216.

Amsterdam, JD., Li, Y., Soeller, I., Rockwell, K., Mao, JJ., and Shults. 2009. "A randomized, double-blind, placebo-controlled trial of oral *Matricaria recutita* extract therapy of generalized anxiety disorder." *J Clin*

Psychopharmacol. 29(4): 378–382.

Amsterdam, JD., Shults, J., Soeller, I., Mao, JJ., Rockwell, K. and Newberg, AB. 2012. "Chamomile (*Matricaria recutita*) May Have Antidepressant Activity in Anxious Depressed Humans - An Exploratory Study." *Altern Ther Health Med.* 18(5): 44-49.

Amsterdam, JD., Li, QS., Xie, SX., & Mao, JJ. 2019. "Putative antidepressant effect of Chamomile *(Matricaria chamomilla L.)* oral extract in subjects with comorbid generalized anxiety disorder and depression." *The Journal of Alternative and Complementary Medicine.*26(9): 815–821.

Bartram, T. 1998. *Bartram's Encyclopedia of Herbal Medicine.* London, England: Constable and Robinson Ltd.

Becker, B., Ulrike Kuhn, U., and Hardewig-Budny, B. 2011. "Double-blind, Randomized Evaluation of Clinical Efficacy and Tolerability of an Apple Pectin-Chamomile Extract in Children with Unspecific Diarrhea." *Arzneimittelforschung.* 56(6): 387-393.

Bone, K. 2003 *A Clinical Guide to Blending Liquid Herbs.* St. Louis, MO: Elsevier Churchill Livingstone.

Bone. K. and Mills, S. 2013. *Principles and Practice of Phytotherapy.* 2nd edition. London, England: Churchill Livingstone.

Braga, F., Santos, A., Bueno, P., Silveira, R., Santos, CB., Bastos, JK., and Carvalho, EC. 2015. "Use of *Chamomilla recutita* in the Prevention and Treatment of Oral Mucositis in Patients Undergoing Hematopoietic Stem Cell Transplantation." *Cancer Nursing.* 38(4): 322–329.

Byrd, JC. And Bresalier, RS. 2000. "Alterations in gastric mucin synthesis by *Helicobacter pylori.*" *World J Gastroentero.* 6(4):475-482.

Carl, W., and Emrich, LS. 1991. "Management of oral mucositis during local radiation and systemic chemotherapy: A study of 98 patients." *The Journal of Prosthetic Dentistry:* 66(3), 361–369.

Castleman, M. 1991. *The Healing Herbs.* Emmaus, PA: Rodale Press.

Chandrashekhar, VM., Ranpariya, VL., Ganapaty, S., Parashar, A., and Muchandi, AA. (2010). "Neuroprotective activity of *Matricaria recutita* Linn against global model of ischemia in rats." *Journal of Ethnopharmacology, 127(3): 645–651.*

Chandrashekhar, VM., Halagali, KS., Nidavani, RB., Shalavadi, MH., Biradar, BS., Biswas, D., and Muchchandi, IS. 2011. "Anti-allergic activity of German chamomile (*Matricaria recutita* L.) in mast cell mediated allergy model." *Journal of Ethnopharmacology.* 137(1): 336–340

Clarke, J. 1982. (reprint of 1901 third edition). *A Dictionary of Practical Materia Medica*. Sussex, England: Health Science Press.

Culpepper, N. 1814. *Culpepper's Complete Herbal*. London, England: Richard Evans.

De La Motte, S., Böse-O'Reilly, S., Heinisch, M., and Harrison, F. 1997. "Double-blind comparison of an apple pectin-chamomile extract preparation with placebo in children with diarrhea." *Arzneimittelforschung*. 47(11): 1247-1249.

Della-Loggia, R., Tubaro, A., Dri, P., Zilli, C., and , Del Negro, P. 1986. "The role of flavonoids in the anti-inflammatory activity of *Chamomilla recutita*." *Prog Clin Biol Res*. 213: 481-484.

Dos Reis, P., Ciol, MA., de Melo, NS., Figueiredo, PT., Leite, AF., and Manzi, N. de M. 2016. "Chamomile infusion cryotherapy to prevent oral mucositis induced by chemotherapy A pilot study." *Supportive Care in Cancer*, 24(10): 4393–4398.

Duke, J. 1985. *Handbook of Medicinal Herbs*, Boca Raton, FL: CRC Press.

---- 2002. *Handbook of Medicinal Herbs*. Bora Raton, FL: CRC Press.

Egan, D., O'Kennedy, R., Moran, E., Cox, D., Prosser, E., and Thornes, R.D. 1990. "The pharmacology, metabolism, analysis, and application of coumarin and coumarin-related compounds." *Drug Metab. Rev*. 22(5): 503-529.

Elhadad, MA., El-Negoumy, E., Taalab, MR., Ibrahim, RS., and Elsaka, RO. 2020. "The effect of topical chamomile in the prevention of chemotherapy-induced oral mucositis: A randomized clinical trial." *Oral Diseases*

Evans, W. 1996. *Trease and Evans' Pharmacognosy*. 14th edition. London, England: WB Saunders Co. Ltd.

Feuer, G. 1974. 3. The Metabolism and Biological Actions of Coumarins. *Progress in Medicinal Chemistry, 85–158.*

Foster, S. 1993. *Herbal Renaissance*. Salt Lake City, UT. Gibbs-Smith Publisher.

Frawley, D. and V. Lad. 2001. *The Yoga of Herbs*. 2nd edition. Twin Lakes, WI : Lotus Press/

Gardner, Z. and McGuffin, M. editors. 2013. *Botanical Safety Handbook*, 2 ed. Boca Raton, FL: CRC Press.

Ghazanfar, SA. 1994. *Handbook of Arabian Medicinal Plants*. Boca Raton, FL: CRC Press.

Glowania, HJ., Raulin, C. and Swoboda, M 1987. "Effect of chamomile on wound healing – A clinical double-blind study". *H+G Zeitschrift für Hautkrankeheiten* 62(17): 1267-1271. Article in German.

Gomes, VTS., Gomes, RNS., Gomes, MS., Joaquim, WM., Lago, EC., Nicolau, RA. 2018. "Effects of *Matricaria recutita* (L.) in the Treatment of Oral Mucositis." *The Scientific World Journal*. Article ID 4392184, 8 pages.

Grieve, M. 1982. *A Modern Herbal*. NY, NY: Dover Publications, Inc. (reprint of 1931 ed.).

Guenther, E. 1952. *The Essential Oils*. Volume V. Malabar, FL: Robert E. Krieger Publishing Co., Inc.

Hardy, K., Buckley, S., Collins, MJ., Estalrrich, A., Brothwell, D., Copeland, L., García-Tabernero, A., García-Vargas, S., de la Rasilla, M., Lalueza-Fox, C., Huguet, R., Bastir, M., Santamaría, D., Madella, M., Wilson, J., Fernández Cortés, J., and Rosas, A. 2012. "Neanderthal medics? Evidence for food, cooking, and medicinal plants entrapped in dental calculus." *Naturwissenschaften,* 99(8), 617–626.

Hardy, K., Buckley, S., and Huffman, M. 2013. "Neanderthal self-medication in context." *Antiquity*. 87(337): 873-878.

Holmes, P. 1989. *The Energetic of Western Herbs*. Boulder, CO: Artemis Press.

Hoffmann, D. 1983. *The New Holistic Herbal*. Rockport, MA: Element Books Limited.

----2003. *Medical Herbalism*. Rochester, VT: Healing Arts Press.

Hutchens, AR. 1973. *Indian Herbology of North America.* Windsor, ON. Canada. Merco.

Jaafarpour, M., Hatefi, M., Khani, A., and Khajavikhan, J. 2015. "Comparative Effect of Cinnamon and Ibuprofen for Treatment of Primary Dysmenorrhea: A Randomized Double- Blind Clinical Trial." *Journal of Clinical and diagnostic research.* 9(4): QC04-07.

Jabri, MA., Aissani, N., Tounsi, H., Sakly, M., Marzouki, L., and Sebai, H. 2017. "Protective effect of chamomile (*Matricaria recutita* L.) decoction extract against alcohol-induced injury in rat gastric mucosa." *Pathophysiology,* 24(1): 1–8.

Jarrahi, M. 2008. "An experimental study of the effects of *Matricaria chamomilla* extract on cutaneous burn wound healing in albino rats." *Natural Product Research*. 22(5): 422–427.

Jarrahi, M., Vafaei, AA., Taherian, AA., Miladi, H., and Rashidi Pour, A. 2010. "Evaluation of topical *Matricaria chamomilla* extract activity on linear incisional wound healing in albino rats." *Natural Product Research,* 24(8): 697–702.

Kay, MA. 1996 *Healing with Plants in the American and Mexican West.* Tucson, AZ: The University of Arizona Press.

Keefe, JR., Mao, JJ., Soeller, I., Li, QS., and Amsterdam, JD. 2016. "Short-term open-label chamomile *(Matricaria chamomilla L.)* therapy of moderate to severe generalized anxiety disorder." *Phytomedicine.* 23(14): 1699–1705

Khayyal, M., El-Ghazaly, M., Kenawy, S., Seif-El-Nasr, M., Mahran, L., Kafafi, Y., and Okpanyi, S. 2011. "Antiulcerogenic Effect of Some Gastrointestinally Acting Plant Extracts and their Combination." *Arzneimittelforschung,* 51(07): 545–553.

Kim, M., Jung, J., Jeong, NY., and Chung, HJ. 2019. "The natural plant flavonoid apigenin is a strong antioxidant that effectively delays peripheral neurodegenerative processes." *Anatomical Science International.* 1-10.

Leclerc, H. 1976. *Précis de phytothérapie.* 5 ed. Paris, France: Masson. (First published in 1922).

Leung, A. and S. Foster. 1996. *Encyclopedia of Common Natural Ingredients used in Food, Drugs and Cosmetics.* 2nd edition. New York, NY: John Wiley & Sons, Inc.

Mabey, R. 1988. *The New Age Herbalist.* New York, NY: MacMillan.

Mao, JJ., Li, QS. Soeller, I., Rockwell, K., Xie, SX., and Amsterdam, JD. 2015. "Long-Term Chamomile Therapy of Generalized Anxiety Disorder: A Study Protocol for a Randomized, Double-Blind, Placebo- Controlled Trial." *Journal of Clinical Trials, 04(05):* 1-20.

Mazokopakis. EE., Vremtzps. GE., Papadakis, JA., Babalis, DE. and Ganotakis, ES. 2005. "Wild chamomile (*Matricaria recutita* L.) mouthwashes in methotrexate-induced oral mucositis." *Phytomedicine* 12: 25–27.

McIntyre, A. 1994. *The Complete Woman's Herbal.* New York, NY. Henry Holt Company.

Menghini, L., Ferrante, C., Leporini, L., Recinella, L., Chiavaroli, A., Leone, S., Pintore, G., Vacca, M., Orlando, G., and Brunetti, L. 2016. "An Hydroalcoholic Chamomile Extract Modulates Inflammatory and Immune Response in HT29 Cells and Isolated Rat Colon." *Phytotherapy Research*, 30(9): 1513–1518.

Menzies-Trull, C. 2003. *Herbal Medicine, Keys to Physiomedicalism including Pharmacopoeia.* Newcastle, England: Faculty of Physiomedical

Herbal Medicine.

Mességué, M. 1975. *Mon herbier de santé.* Paris, France: Laffont.

Moshfegh, Z., and Setorki, M. 2017. "Neuroprotective effect of *Matricaria chamomilla* extract on motor dysfunction induced by transient global cerebral ischemia and reperfusion in rats." *Zahedan J Res Med Sci.* 19(9): e10927.

Mushtaq, Z., Sadeer, NB., Hussain, M., Mahwish, Alsagaby, SA., Imran, M., Mumtaz, T., Umar, M., Tauseef, A., Al Abdulmonem, W., Tufail, T., Al Jbawi, E. and Mahomoodally, MF. 2023. "Therapeutical properties of apigenin: a review on the experimental evidence and basic mechanisms." *International Journal of Food Properties,* 26:1: 1914-1939.

Niazi, A., and Moradi, M. 2021. "The Effect of Chamomile on Pain and Menstrual Bleeding in Primary Dysmenorrhea: A Systematic Review.*" IJCBNM.* 9(3):174-186.

Nickell, JM. 1976. *J.M. Nickell's Botanical Ready Reference.* Lakemont, GA: CSA Press.

Paris, RR., and Moyse, H. 1971. *Matière Médicale.* Paris, France, Masson et Cie.

Pelkonen, O., Raunio, H., and Pasanen, M. 1997. "The metabolism of coumarin." In O'Kennedy, K., and R.D. Thornes, ed. *Coumarins: Biology, applications and mode of action.* Hoboken, NJ: Willey.

Petronilho, S., Maraschin,M., Coimbra, MA, and , Rocha, SM. 2012. "In vitro and in vivo studies of natural products: A challenge for their valuation. The case study of chamomile (*Matricaria recutita* L.)." *Industrial Crops and Products* 40: 1– 12.

Ramos-e-Silva , M., Ferreira, AF., Bibas, R., and Carneiro, S. 2006. "Clinical evaluation of fluid extract of *Chamomilla recutita* for oral aphthae." *J Drugs Dermatol.* 5(7): 612-617.

Romm, A. 2010. *Botanical Medicine for Women's Health.* St. Louis, MO. Churchill Livingstone Elsevier.

Saadatmand, S., Zohroudi, F. and Tangestani, H. 2024. "The Effect of Oral Chamomile on Anxiety: A Systematic Review of Clinical Trials." *Clin Nutr Res.* 13(2): 139-147.

Safayhi, H., Sabieraj, J., Sailer, ER., and Ammon, H. 1994. *"*Chamazulene: An Antioxidant-Type Inhibitor of Leukotriene B4 Formation." *Planta Medica,* 60(05), 410–441.

Schaffner, W. 1992. *Les plantes médicinales et leur propriétés.* Lausanne,

Switzerland : Delachaux et Niestlé.

Schulz, V., R. Hansel, M. Blumenthal and V. Tyler. 2004. *Rational Phytotherapy, A Reference guide for Physicians and Pharmacists.* 5th edition. Berlin, Germany: Springer.

Seyyedi, SA., Sanatkhani, M., Pakfetrat, A. and Olyaee, P. 2014. "The therapeutic effects of chamomilla tincture mouthwash on oral aphthae: A Randomized Clinical Trial." *J Clin Exp Dent.* 6(5): 535-538.

Shabani, F., Narenji, F., Vakilian, K., Zareian, MA., Bozorgi, M,, Bioos, S., and Nejatbakhsh, F. 2022. "Comparing the Effect of Chamomile and Mefenamic Acid on Primary Dysmenorrhea Symptoms and Menstrual Bleeding: A Randomized Clinical Trial." *The Open Public Health Journal.* 15: 1-10.

Shabanloei, R. Ahmadi, F., Vaez, J., Ansarin, K., Hajizadeh, E., Javadzadeh, Y., et al. 2009. "Alloprinol, chamomile and normal saline mouthwashes for the prevention of chemotherapy induced stomatitis." *J Clin Diagn Res.* 3:1537–1542.

Skenderi, G. 2003. *Herbal Vade Mecum.* Rutherford, NJ: Herbacy Press.

Srivastava, JK., Pandey, M., and Gupta, S. 2009. "Chamomile, a novel and selective COX-2 inhibitor with anti-inflammatory activity." *Life Sciences,* 85(19-20), 663–669.

Srivastava, JK., Shankar, E. and Gupta, S. 2010. "Chamomile: A herbal medicine of the past with bright future." *Mol Med Report.* 3(6): 895–901.

Stansbury, J. 2018. *Herbal Formularies for Health Professionals Vol. 3. Endocrinology.* White River Junction, VT: Chelsea Green Publishing.

Szelenyi, I., Isaac, O., and Thiemer, K. 1979. "Pharmacological experiments with compounds of chamomile III. Experimental studies of the ulceroprotective effects of chamomile [article in German]." *Planta Med.* 35(3): 218-227.

Tadbir, AA., Pourshahidi, S., Ebrahimi, H., Hajipour, Z., Memarzade, MR., and Shirazian, S. 2015. "The effect of *Matricaria chamomilla* (chamomile) extract in Orabase on minor aphthous stomatitis, a randomized clinical trial." *Journal of Herbal Medicine.* 5(2): 71-76.

Trousseau, A. and Pidoux, H. 1877. *Traité de thérapeutique et de matière médicale.* Tome 2. Paris, France: P. Asselin.

Tyler, ML. 1952. *Homoeopathic Drug Pictures.* Devon, England: Health Science Press.

Tyler, V. 1993. *The Honest Herbal.* 3rd edition. Binghampton, NY: The Haworth Press.

Uphof, J.C. 1968. *Dictionary of Economic Plants*. New York, NY. Stechert-Harner Service Agency, Inc.

Valnet, J. 1992. *Phytothérapie*. 6 ed. Paris, France: Maloine.

Van Hellemont, J. 1986. *Compendium de Phytothérapie*. Brussels, Belgium: Association Pharmaceutique Belge.

Viola, H., Wasowski, C., Levi de Stein, M., Wolfman, C., Silveira, R., Dajas, F., Medina, JH., and Paladini. AC. 1995. "Apigenin, a component of *Matricaria recutita* flowers, is a central benzodiazepine receptors-ligand with anxiolytic effects." *PlantaMed*. 61: 213-216.

Weiss, R. 1988. *Herbal Medicine*. Beaconsfield, England: Beaconsfield Publishers Ltd.

Wichtl, M. (Ed.) 2004. *Herbal Drugs and Phytopharmaceuticals*. 3 ed. Boca Raton, FL: CRC Press.

Wikifarmer, 2024. "German Chamomile Essential Oil Yield." Accessed on 7/26/2024 at https://wikifarmer.com/german-chamomile-essential-oil-yield/.

Wren, RB. 1988. *Potter's New Cyclopaedia of Botanical Drugs and Preparations*. Revised by E. Williamson. Essex, England: The C.W. Daniel Company Limited.

Zargaran, A., Borhani-Haghighi, A., Faridi, P., Daneshamouz, S., Kordafshari, G., and Mohagheghzadeh, A. 2014. "Potential effect and mechanism of action of topical chamomile (Matricaria chammomila L.) oil on migraine headache: A medical hypothesis." Medical Hypotheses, 83(5): 566–569.

Zargaran, A., Borhani-Haghighi, A., Salehi-Marzijarani, M., Faridi, P., Daneshamouz, S., Azadi, A., Sadeghpour, H., Sakhteman, A. and Mohagheghzadeh, A. 2018. "Evaluation of the effect of topical chamomile (Matricaria chamomilla L.) oleogel as pain relief in migraine without aura: a randomized, double-blind, placebo-controlled, crossover study." Neurological Sciences, 39(8): 1345–1353.

Zimmermann, M., Johnson, H., McGuffin, M. and Applequist, W. 2023. *AHPA's Herbs of Commerce*, 3 ed. Silver Spring, MD: American Herbal Products Association.

Daniel Gagnon, Medical Herbalist, MS, RH (AHG) is a French-Canadian originally from Northern Ontario who relocated to Santa Fe, NM in 1979. For over 45 years he worked in the herbal medicine consumer product manufacturing sector and was the owner of Herbs, Etc., Inc. He has been a practicing Medical Herbalist since 1976. Daniel is the author of *The Practical Guide to Herbal Medicines*, a book designed to provide herbal health care options. With Amadea Morningstar, he is also the co-author of *Breathe Free*, a book on healing the respiratory system. He regularly teaches herbal therapeutics both nationally and internationally. Daniel retained ownership of Herbs, Etc., the herbal medicine retail store located in Santa Fe, NM. Daniel can be reached at botandan@aol.com or daniel.gagnon@froggysmeadow.com.

Besides their medicinal virtues, chamomile blooms attract pollinators and are companion plants to many crops. *Susan Belsinger*

Chamomile in the Home Apothecary

Carol Little

Chamomile has a wide range of practical uses for everyday complaints, and because it is a mild herb, its applications are reputedly safe with virtually no known risk of side effects, except for those allergic to Asteraceae. This herb is one of the most famous medicinal plants in history and has been used for centuries.

Both German and Roman chamomile have small daisy-like blossoms which grow on delicate stalks with feathery foliage. Blooms arrive in May and may last until September in northern climates. The plant will continue to bloom profusely, as long as we keep harvesting the flowers.

Chamomile Highlights

There are dozens of attributes: anti-viral, anti-inflammatory, antimicrobial, antispasmodic, antiseptic, carminative, cholagogue, diaphoretic, digestive aid, emmenagogue, febrifuge, immuno-stimulant, nervine, respiratory, and vulnerary.

Chamomile is a super-star!

There is *more*, but I tend to think of chamomile *mostly* to support the nervous system, digestive system, respiratory system, and to an extent, the musculo-skeletal system.

Chamomile is among the mildest of the nervine herbs. It can help with stress, induce calmness, and offers gentle help to overcome anxiety and depression.

Some people may need a stronger nervine, such as motherwort or skullcap, to help them with these issues, but for others, chamomile will work well.

Chamomile is also one of the gentlest allies that can give us a good night's sleep. Many people who don't otherwise use herbal medicine will try chamomile tea precisely for this reason.

Like many nervous system supporters, it can help to relax both our mind and muscles, which can alleviate emotional imbalances, physical pain and insomnia.

Chamomile can actually help with pain anywhere in the body, including headaches, migraines, and menstrual cramps

Chamomile treats a wide range of upper respiratory conditions, including asthma, bronchitis, coughs, wheezing, sinusitis and sore throats. I predominantly use chamomile to help with runny nose and hay fever symptoms.

Chamomile is an antispasmodic and, as such, can help to calm all muscles, including the involuntary ones. This allows us to soothe and even stop irritating coughs. We can soothe colic in children, as well.

Chamomile can relax the mucous membranes and heal inflammation. This enables chamomile to treat gastritis, ulcerative colitis, stomach ulcers, and IBS symptoms. Overall, chamomile can help us to alleviate many inflammatory conditions of the gastrointestinal tract and respiratory system.

Chamomile, both carminative and anti-nausea, can help to lower the acidity in the stomach and can be an excellent remedy for heartburn. Known to inhibit the *Helicobacter pylori bacteria,* which can contribute to heartburn in some folks or cause stomach ulcers, chamomile can be very powerful. Chamomile further aids digestion by gently stimulating bile production, which helps our body to assimilate the lipids (fats) in our meals.

Chamomile is quite well known as a gentle healer of cuts, scrapes and stings. Chamomile is an effective antiseptic, so it can clean wounds and keep them safe from infection in addition to facilitating healing. A washcloth dipped in warm chamomile tea can cleanse and relieve soreness.

Chamomile also treats eczema, and recent studies have found it more effective than corticosteroid creams. Studies have also confirmed its use as a *woundwort*, a plant that can speed the healing of wounds. Many women use it to treat cracked nipples.

Officinæ Ca=
momillam per
peram vocant,
& pro vero
Chamæmelo in
vsum recipiūt.
Germani erro
rem Officina=
rum sequētes
Chamill.
Brabanti
Camille.
Galli Camo
mille vocant.

hamæmelum
vlgare Leuchant.
Diosc. Pin. Anth
is vulgatior, sive Cha:
mæmilla - Ad.

Cat. Chamamille -

Chamomile has been used medicinally since before recorded history and is featured in medieval herbals. *Matricaria chamomilla* L. Dodonaeus, R., *Stirp. Hist. Comment.* 1553-1554. *www.plantillustrations.org*

Because it is so gentle, chamomile is often the first herb a parent will choose for an infant. Our children can drink chamomile tea for a good night's sleep, to soothe a tummy ache, or to help with a cold or flu.

Of course, the preparation also affects the strength of the remedy. A weak tea is gentler than a strong infusion or a tincture, and chamomile works well in all these forms.

While German chamomile is used most often, Roman chamomile has some similar properties but its use is contraindicated during pregnancy. Gentle as chamomile is, it can cause allergic reactions in some people with ragweed allergies. Many people with ragweed allergies can enjoy chamomile without problems, but some cannot. Obviously, if you're allergic to chamomile, you'll do better to use other herbs instead.

Herbs can potentiate other herbs and medications that treat the same conditions. I tend to avoid giving therapeutic doses of nervines, for example, when an individual is taking prescription sedatives. A cup of chamomile tea in the evenings is "food." However, a tincture combination containing chamomile and stronger nervous system herbs has the ability to "pump up" the drug's effects. If we are using herbs this way, it's best to pay close attention and proceed carefully and cautiously.

A favourite chamomile tea blend

1 part chamomile
1 part rose petals
1 part holy basil
1 part lemon balm
1/2 part passion flower
1/2 part spearmint
1/4 part orange peel
Pinch of licorice root, optional

Combine all ingredients and store them in a cool, dry place. To brew, use 1 tablespoon of this blend per cup of water. Pour boiling water over the herbs, cover with a tight lid, and allow to steep for 10 to 20 minutes. Strain and enjoy!

This does include herbs that have sedative qualities, so don't drink it and operate heavy machinery until you know how the tea will affect you. Do not drink this tea if you are taking other prescription sedative medications. Omit the licorice root if you have high blood pressure.

Chamomile's abundant useful actions make it a wonderful herbal choice for every member of the family. I sincerely hope that this gentle, yet very powerful, medicine brightens and strengthens you and your family!

Carol Little, R.H is a traditional herbalist in Toronto, Cananda, where she has had a private practice for over 20 years. She loves to write about how we can incorporate herbs into our daily lives. Her easy-to-digest weekly blog posts offer quick takeaway ideas to help readers to feel their best. https://studiobotanica.com

Carol is a current professional and past board member of the Ontario Herbalists Association. She combines her love of travel and passion for all things green and enjoys writing about both. Carol has written for *Vitality Magazine* for many years. She is a regular contributor to the IHA annual *Herb of the Year* book. She is a proud participant in the much-loved *FIRE CIDER 101 Zesty Recipes for Health-Boosting Remedies* by Rosemary Gladstar and friends.

Carol's current project is a fun-filled "deep dive" into one herb each month—it's called HerbGals and is a creative and interactive way to learn about the many gifts and practical ways that we can embrace the green world. Herb enthusiasts, herbalists, gardeners, and those with culinary interests share and learn from each other!

For more information:
https://studiobotanica.teachable.com/p/herbgals
https://www.facebook.com/studiobotanica
https://instagram.com/studiobotanica

Roman chamomile

Chamaemelum nobile, Burnett. *Plantae utiliores*, 1847.

Captivating Chamomile:
A Tale of Two Varieties

Dorene Petersen

Chamomile herb and essential oil are cornerstones in herbalists' and aromatherapists' apothecaries, celebrated for their soothing and therapeutic properties. From easing stress to calming skin irritations, chamomile has woven itself into the fabric of natural healing, and its appeal is nothing new. Since the days of ancient Egypt, this humble flower has enchanted civilizations—rumor has it that Cleopatra herself may have indulged in its calming embrace after a long day of ruling. Fast forward to today, and chamomile's magic continues to captivate.

In my quest to source certified organic, sustainably produced chamomile herb and essential oil, I undertook a fascinating journey through Hungary, Nepal, and South Korea, delving into the intricacies of local chamomile cultivation and production practices. My findings were both encouraging and alarming—while each region boasts its own traditional cultivation methods, pesticide-laden soils and improper handling during harvest in some areas risk contaminating and losing the plant's precious dried herb and essential oil content. This discovery sheds light on the fragility of this gentle ancient herb and highlights the vital role of expert care in every step of its cultivation and processing. Without it, we risk diminishing the very essence that has soothed humanity for millennia.

Yet behind its gentle demeanor lies a compelling tale of two distinct varieties: the soothing Blue chamomile (*Matricaria recutita*) (also known as German chamomile; read on to hear the story behind this common name change) and the robust Roman chamomile (*Chamaemelum nobile*). Among the different varieties of chamomile, Blue chamomile and Roman chamomile are the most prominent. Though they share a rich heritage, these two herbs are worlds apart in their unique qualities, each offering their own brand of botanical magic.

Chamomile Maroc, or Moroccan Chamomile (*Ormenis mixta* or *Ormenis multicaulis*), is a third variety of chamomile, but it is botanically and therapeutically different from the traditional chamomile species. While it is often marketed as "chamomile" (especially the essential oil), it's not a true chamomile like the Blue or Roman varieties. Moroccan Chamomile is commonly used in the perfume and cosmetics industries and its therapeutic properties are milder compared to Blue and Roman chamomile. Despite being a different genus than either Blue or Roman, it is still appreciated for its soothing and anti-inflammatory effects, though it's less commonly used in medicinal herbalism or aromatherapy.

This article delves into the botanical characteristics, cultivation, uses, medicinal benefits, and safety considerations for both Blue and Roman chamomile, focusing on what makes each variety unique.

Botanical Characteristics

Blue Chamomile

The word *chamomile* is derived from the Greek words *khamai*, meaning "on the ground," and *mēlon*, meaning "apple," a fitting description of the plant's apple-like fragrance.

With their precision in language, the Greeks aptly captured the essence of the humble yet fragrant flower of Blue chamomile. Although commonly known as German chamomile, Blue chamomile has become ubiquitous, growing in many regions around the world. A highly respected and knowledgeable Hungarian farmer and distiller of Blue chamomile (our source for therapeutically viable essential oil for ACHS.edu and the Apothecary-Shoppe.com) graciously informed me, during a visit to his distillery and enchanting chamomile fields, that "German chamomile" is a misnomer, as the plant is cultivated in many parts of the world. He prefers the term "Blue chamomile," which I now choose to adopt, recognizing and honoring the diversity of its global origins.

Blue chamomile, also known by its Latin name *Matricaria recutita*, belongs to the Asteraceae family, previously known as Compositae. This annual plant is characterized by its erect, round stems that can grow 1.5 to 3 feet high. The leaves are divided and thread-like, with only a few leaves on each stem. The plant produces daisy-like flowers with a hollow conical center about an inch across. A notable feature is the tiny scales between each two florets, which, although difficult to see, help distinguish Blue chamomile from other species. The aroma of Blue chamomile flowers is similar to Roman chamomile, but less aromatic and much stronger, with a distinctly bitter taste that is more pronounced than its Roman counterpart.

Roman Chamomile

Roman chamomile, scientifically known as *Chamaemelum nobile*, also belongs to the Asteraceae family. It is often called Roman chamomile, garden chamomile, or camomile. This herb is a low-growing perennial with hairy stems that form a ground cover. Its fine, feathery, and thread-like leaves complement the plant's single or double daisy-like flowers, which have a solid yellow center and white florets on a long, erect stalk. The strong apple scent and pleasant aromatic taste distinguish Roman chamomile flowers and leaves.

Both varieties of chamomile showcase an intriguing feature: surface trichomes, which can be found on the leaves, flowers, and sometimes even the roots of certain herbs. While invisible to the naked eye, under a microscope, these specialized cells appear as either delicate hairlike structures or tiny cellular puffballs, as illustrated in the images. These trichomes play a vital role in the plant's survival, storing and releasing volatile compounds, and they are also the source of the precious essential oils that end up in your bottle. Because trichomes are so fragile, gentle harvesting, precise drying, and careful storage are crucial to preserving as many of them as possible, resulting in a product that is not only rich in aroma but also packed with therapeutic potency.

Isn't it amazing how something so small holds such incredible power?

Still confused about how to spot the difference? Here are a few more clues. Roman chamomile and Blue chamomile can be easily distinguished by aroma, taste, and a careful inspection of the stems and flowers.

Roman chamomile is a perennial with scented foliage that smells extremely strong, like green Granny Smith apples. Blue chamomile is an annual, and the foliage has no aroma. Roman chamomile has slightly hairy stems, while blue chamomile has smooth ones. Roman chamomile flowers sit singly atop the stem, while Blue chamomile is on divided stems in a comb-like arrangement. Another distinct characteristic is the cone in the center of Blue chamomile, which distinctly domes out, whereas Roman chamomile is flat.

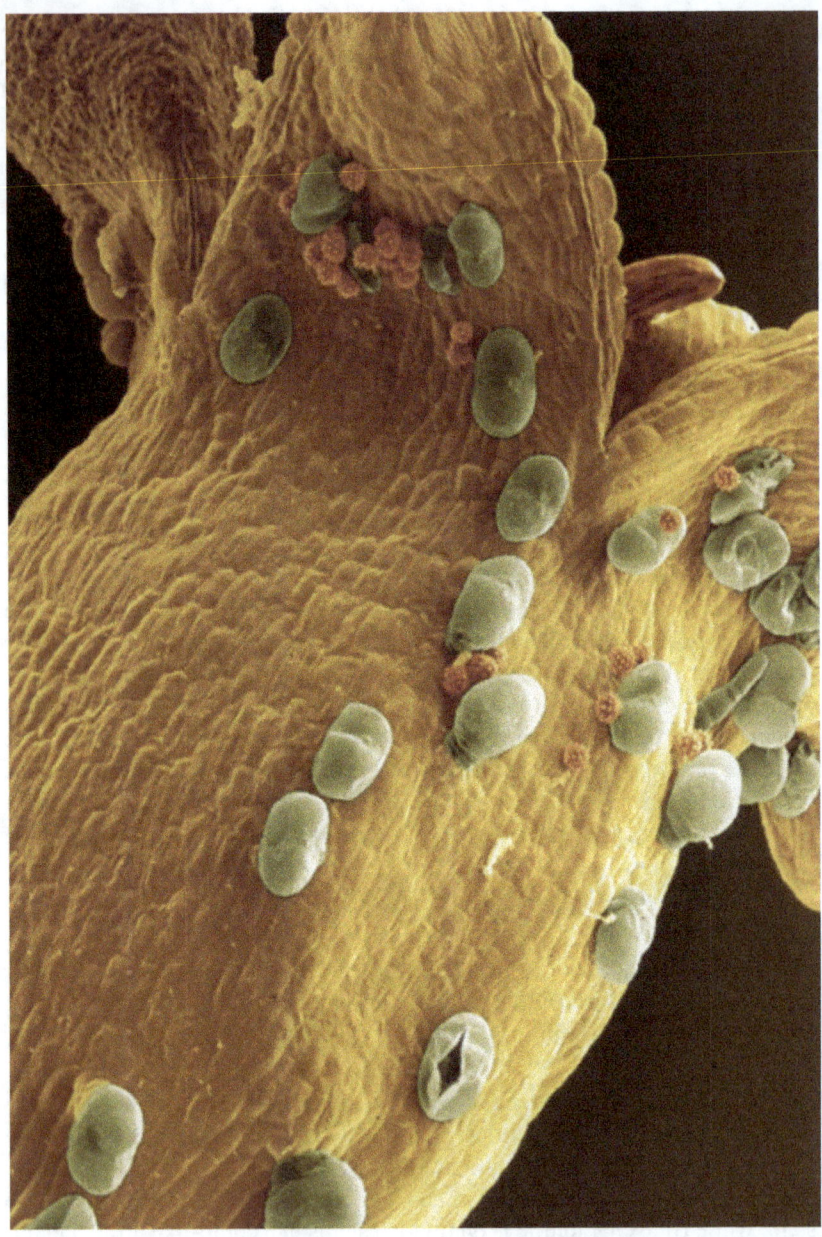

Roman chamomile floret close-up microscopic view. *Svoboda, K. & Svoboda, T. (2000). Secretory Structures of Aromatic and Medicinal Plants.* Knighton, UK: Microscopix Publications. *Reproduced with permission.*

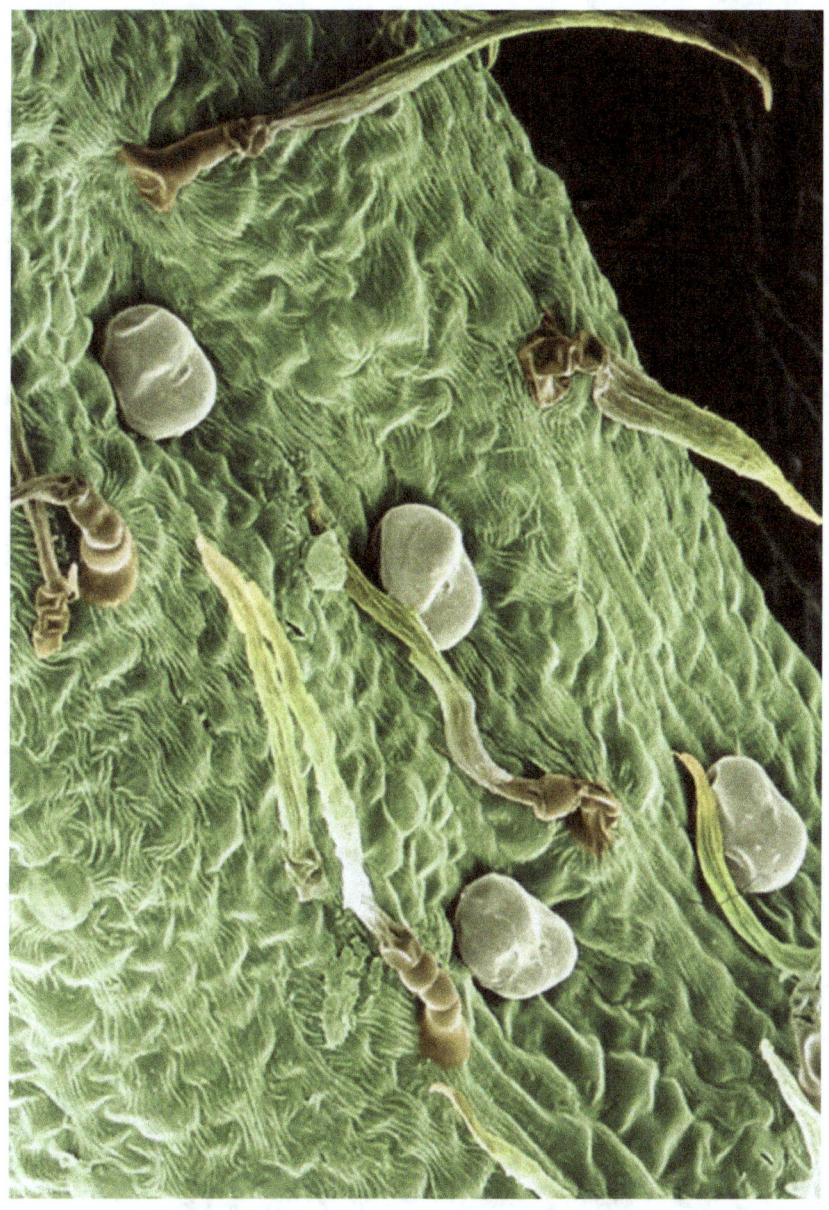

Blue chamomile: upper leaf surface with sessile secretory glands and nonsecretory trichomes. *Svoboda, K. & Svoboda, T. (2000). Secretory Structures of Aromatic and Medicinal Plants.* Knighton, UK: Microscopix Publications. *Reproduced with permission.*

Here is a quick-glance reference chart:

Roman chamomile (Chamaemelum nobile)	Perennial	Slightly hairy	Sit atop the stem; apple aroma and taste much stronger than Blue chamomile	Flat	Strong aroma of Granny Smith apples
Blue chamomile Matricaria recutita)	Annual	Smooth	On divided stems in a comb-like pattern; apple aroma and more bitter taste	Domes out	No Aroma

Important Note About Chamomile Research

Be cautious when reading published research about chamomile. Many research articles use the term chamomile and do not distinguish between *C. nobile* or *M. recutita*. We encourage you to read research very carefully with a focus on the scientific or Latin name and, if necessary, contact the author(s). Also, note that there has been a change in the scientific names of Roman and Blue chamomiles. Latin binomials change as the field of plant nomenclature is in constant flux. Blue chamomile has changed from *Matricaria chamomilla* (L.) to *Matricaria recutita* (L.). Roman chamomile has changed from *Anthemis nobilis* (L.) to *Chamaemelum nobile* (L.)

Roman chamomile, *Chamaemelum nobile*. Karlsruhe Botanical Garden, Germany. *www.commons.wikimedia.org*

Blue chamomile (*Matricaria recutita*) growing in Hungary.
Dorene Petersen

Cultivation and Harvesting

Blue chamomile thrives in sandy loam soil with ample moisture. Propagation is typically from tiny seeds that should be planted very shallowly. Adding potassium-rich organic compost can encourage flowering. The harvesting process is labor-intensive, requiring careful selection of flowers at nearly full bloom for optimal medicinal use.

On the other hand, Roman chamomile prefers acidic soils with ample organic matter and a moist but well-drained location. It is less widely cultivated than Blue chamomile. Harvesting involves removing the flowers and stem tips when the flowers are in full bloom, and the petals begin to lie back from the center.

In Korea, Roman chamomile can be found sustainably cultivated among other medicinal botanicals such as lavender, nasturtium, plantain, echinacea, and peony. Enjoy this virtual field trip from my visit to a Korean lavender and chamomile farm at 3,000 feet above sea level to appreciate the intensive harvesting process for chamomile: ACHS.edu Dorene Petersen Harvesting Chamomile in Korea (URL https://www.youtube.com/watch?v=WmY3-j2ZAWw&t=1s).

Storage

Like all herbs and essential oils, chamomile should be stored very carefully in well-filled, tightly closed containers at a cool temperature and protected from light. Contact with air will cause both evaporation and deterioration. Exposure to oxygen also causes essential oils to oxidize. This causes safety issues. Botanicals lose their medicinal potency and oxidized essential oil constituents can trigger allergic reactions.

Household Uses

Blue chamomile is a popular ingredient in herbal teas, often consumed as a nightcap to promote restful sleep. The dried or fresh flowers can also be used in salads, providing a good source of calcium. Its pleasant taste and aroma make it a versatile addition to various culinary and household applications.

Roman chamomile, similarly, is used in teas for relaxation and as a hair rinse for blonde hair, adding highlights. The fresh flowers can be used in salads as a rich source of calcium, adding flavor and nutritional value.

Active Constituents

Let's explore what makes these two similar yet distinct chamomiles such powerful wellness tools.

Blue chamomile contains varying amounts of volatile essential oil rich in the constituent chamazulene. Chamazulene is also found in yarrow (*Achillea millefolium*) and wormwood (*Artemisia absinthium*). Chamazulene is responsible for its notable anti-inflammatory effects, alleviates painful discomfort, acts as a wound healer, and offers antispasmodic and antimicrobial benefits. Chamazulene is a powerful anti-inflammatory compound and is often found in skincare products for its soothing effect. During steam distillation, another compound called matricin transforms into chamazulene. Matricin is said to be an even more potent anti-inflammatory than chamazulene itself. Alpha-bisabolol is also present in Blue chamomile and is sometimes present in Roman chamomile essential oils.The presence of chamazulene alerts you to the need for careful storage for both chamomile herb and essential oil. Chamazulene and alpha-bisabolol are both unstable.

The essential oil also contains farnesene, a fragrant component found in hops (*Humulus lupulus*) and apple skins, along with alpha-bisabolol and trans-en-yn-dicycloether. Both alpha-bisabolol and trans-en-yn-dicycloether have shown anti-inflammatory, antiseptic, and antimicrobial properties in lab studies involving rats. In particular, alpha-bisabolol demonstrated anti-ulcer activity, helping prevent ulcers caused by stress, ethanol, or medications like indomethacin, a nonsteroidal anti-inflammatory prescription drug.

Blue chamomile herb is rich in flavonoids, including apigenin and apiin (found in parsley *Petroselinum crispum* and celery *Apium graveolens*), as well as rutin, which helps strengthen fragile capillaries and benefits the circulatory system and heart.

Other important constituents include luteolin (a glycoside), umbelliferone (a coumarin with antifungal and antibacterial properties), plant acids, azulene, fatty acids, amino acids, choline (also found in dandelion), and varying amounts of minerals like calcium and potassium.

The three key esters in Roman Chamomile oil are isobutyl angelate, 2-methylbutyl angelate, and methallyl angelate, which are known for their ability to relieve muscle spasms.

Roman Chamomile oil also contains varying amounts of chamazulene.

Other important constituents provide additional support such as pinene (a terpene), farnesol and nerolidol (alcohols), pinocarvone (a ketone), and 1,8 cineol (an oxide). Notably, 1,8 cineol is a potent antiseptic and antimicrobial agent.

Therapeutic Actions and Medicinal Uses

Blue chamomile boasts a plethora of medicinal properties. As an antioxidant, it protects cells from damage by free radicals, which are unstable molecules that can cause cell damage. Its antimicrobial properties inhibit the growth of microorganisms such as bacteria and fungi. Blue chamomile also acts as an antidepressant and anti-anxiety agent, reducing symptoms by affecting brain chemicals that influence mood. Its anti-inflammatory properties help reduce inflammation and soothe irritated tissues. Additionally, it has antidiarrheal effects, alleviating diarrhea by calming the digestive tract.

Blue chamomile also promotes angiogenesis, forming new blood vessels, which is important for wound healing and recovery. It shows potential in inhibiting the growth of cancer cells, acting as an anticarcinogenic agent. Blue chamomile essential oil showed positive activity in this study against three human cancer cell lines: lung, colon, and breast.

Anticonvulsant

Furthermore, it protects the liver, known as a hepatoprotective effect, and helps manage blood sugar levels, providing antidiabetic benefits.

Recent studies have reinforced these findings. For instance, a 2022 review highlighted the anti-inflammatory, antioxidant, analgesic, antimicrobial, hepatoprotective, anti-allergic, anticancer, and anti-hypertensive properties of Blue (German) chamomile. Another study confirmed its potent antioxidant activity and significant anticancer effects against liver cancer cells.

The most well-known effect of Blue chamomile is its calming and sleep-promoting properties. Clinical studies have shown its effectiveness in reducing anxiety and promoting sleep in elderly populations and postnatal women. It has also been demonstrated to reduce anxiety in women during childbirth. Blue chamomile infusion is recommended to support flatulence, travel sickness, nasal mucous membrane inflammation, and nervous diarrhea. It is effective for gastrointestinal spasms and digestive tract inflammation, including the mouth. Mouth ulcers, particularly those associated with chemotherapy or radiation treatment, respond well to chamomile mouthwashes. Another alternative is to dab the essential oil on mouth ulcers with a Q-tip for soothing relief.

Blue chamomile is also known for its wound-healing properties. Topical application of chamomile has been reported to be more effective than 1% topical hydrocortisone ointment in managing peristomal skin lesions, which are skin irritations around a stoma. In Italy, it is commonly used to soothe skin inflammations such as psoriasis, acne and rashes, and as an eyewash for conjunctivitis (pink eye). The Blue chamomile ointment found in the formulas is recommended for any dry, inflamed skin issues.

Additionally, Blue chamomile provides support before and during menstruation. Clinical reports indicate that it can reduce the severity of premenstrual syndrome (PMS), dysmenorrhea (painful menstruation), and menstrual bleeding. Topical application of chamomile essential oil has been found helpful for relieving pain and improving physical function in patients with knee osteoarthritis.

Roman chamomile, on the other hand, is recommended as an aromatic bitter, which stimulates digestion by increasing saliva and digestive juices, and a spasmolytic, which relaxes muscle spasms. It is also known as a mild sedative, helping to induce relaxation, reduce anxiety, and calm and tranquilize nerves. A study with 56 ICU patients showed the patients who inhaled an aromatherapy blend of lavender, Roman chamomile, and neroli essential oils slept better after surgery and had lower levels of anxiety. Similarly, literature reviews indicate its potential in acute care settings for the support of "wounds and ulcers to insomnia and stress."

Traditionally, it is used for soothing various stomach ailments, such as sluggish digestion, flatulence, and pain in the upper abdomen after eating. Roman chamomile has also demonstrated hypoglycemic effects, helping to lower blood sugar levels.

Roman chamomile's vasorelaxant properties help relax the blood vessels, improving circulation and reducing blood pressure. It has been shown to have broncho-relaxant activity, making it potentially supportive for bronchial asthma. Topically, it can be applied to boils and abscesses as a compress to draw out inflammation. It also has antibacterial properties, inhibiting bacteria involved in periodontitis (gum disease) and preventing biofilm formation on surfaces.

Safety Considerations

Blue chamomile is generally recognized as safe (GRAS) when used orally in amounts commonly found in foods. However, it may cause allergic reactions in individuals sensitive to the Asteraceae family. Caution is advised during pregnancy and when taking anticoagulants like warfarin due to its coumarin content, which can thin the blood.

Roman chamomile is also generally recognized as safe when used appropriately. It is advised to avoid use during pregnancy due to its potential abortifacient effects. Like Blue chamomile, it may cause allergic reactions in individuals sensitive to the Asteraceae family.

Dosage and Usage

For Blue chamomile, an infusion can be prepared using one ounce of dried flowers and one pint of purified water, consumed up to three times daily. Three to 5 drops of essential oil can be added to a bath for a calming effect.

For Roman chamomile, a tea can be made by steeping one ounce of flowers in one pint of purified water, consumed up to three times daily. The essential oil can also be used similarly to German chamomile, with 3 to 5 drops in a bath for relaxation.

Formulas

Formula Information

Shelf life of the essential oils is generally one year if stored correctly. Always conduct an organoleptic assessment and skin patch test before use. Be sure to label and date formulations and store in a cool, dark location.

Ingredients for Blue or Roman Chamomile ointment. *Dorene Petersen*

Blue or Roman Chamomile Ointment

Sweet almond oil: 2 ounces
Beeswax unbleached: 1/4 ounce or use the vegan alternative called
Candelilla
Blue or Roman Chamomile essential oil: 20 drops
Bergamot essential *Citrus aurantium* var. *bergamia* essential oil: 10 drops
Geranium *Pelargonium graveolens* essential oil: 8 drops

Warm the almond oil over a double boiler and add the grated beeswax or
Candelilla. Stir until the wax is dissolved, then add the essential oils. Cool
before placing in jars, and to avoid condensation, leave it to completely cool
before putting on the lid.

Blue or Roman Chamomile Emulsified Ointment

Beeswax (or vegan Candelilla): 1/2 ounce
Sweet almond oil: 1 ounce
Filtered water (warmed): 7 ounces
Blue or Roman Chamomile essential oil: 10 drops

Preparing an emulsified ointment is a little like making mayonnaise, as one
who cooks can attest. It is quite a delicate process, and the key points are
the temperature of the oil/wax mixture and the water. They should both be
lukewarm, between 98°F and 105°F. The key is to have two thermometers,
one in the water and one in the oil, to make sure both are the same temperature.
It is also important not to overblend. As soon as emulsification begins, turn
the immersion blender or blender off. If you blend by hand, stop whisking.

Preparing the Base

Melt the beeswax and almond oil in a water bath or a double boiler. Never
place on direct heat. Note: Take care that no water gets into the beeswax/oil
mix while melting.

Remove the mixture from the heat and allow it to cool until lukewarm. Test
the temperature by dipping a spoon into the mixture; it should start to coat
the spoon.

Warm the filtered water to about the same temperature as the oil\wax mix (they should be very close in temperature). Test the temperature of the filtered water by dropping on the inner wrist. It should feel slightly lukewarm.

Emulsification Procedure

Slowly but continuously add the warm, filtered water to the warm beeswax/oil base while briskly beating continuously (manually with a whisk, but an immersion blender works much better, or use a blender, but on a very low setting). The emulsification process will take some time, so be patient, but when it happens, it happens immediately.

STOP as soon as it starts to emulsify!

Add the essential oil and gently blend by hand with a spatula. STOP as soon it appears combined. Note: It is helpful to pre-measure the essential oil beforehand to avoid having to count drops into the emulsified mixture.

Pour into jar(s) and cool.

Indigestion/Loss of Appetite Rub

Blue chamomile or Roman chamomile essential oil: 5 drops
Bergamot *Citrus aurantium* var. *bergamia* essential oil: 3 drops
Ginger *Zingiber officinale* essential oil: 3 drops
Grapeseed oil: 1 ounce

Instructions: Blend oils and massage the stomach and intestinal area in a clockwise direction using small, circular movements. Avoid direct sunlight on massaged areas when using this blend.

Blood Flow Support

Cypress *Cupressus sempervirens* essential oil: 15 drops
Blue or Roman chamomile essential oil 10 drops
Bergamot *Citrus aurantium* var. *bergamia* oil: 5 drops
Rose hip seed *Rosa canina fructus* oil: 2 ounces
Vitamin E oil: 1/4 ounce

Instructions: Blend the oils and massage gently into enlarged veins, avoiding bruised or swollen areas. Avoid direct sunlight on massaged areas when using this blend.

Infused Oil for Muscle and Joint Pain

Roman Chamomile flowers (dried): 1 ounce
Organic Peanut oil: 1 pint

Instructions: Mix in a wide-mouth jar with a non-metal lid. Leave in a warm but sunless spot for two weeks. Shake frequently, ensuring all the flowers are beneath the surface of the oil. After two weeks, strain through a coffee filter or four layers of unbleached cheesecloth. Ensure no plant material is left in the oil, which can promote spoilage. Essential oil of Roman chamomile can also be added to the final product. You can also add rosemary essential oil for an extra boost of pain relief. Use up to 12 drops of essential oil (2% dilution).

Facial Oil

Roman Chamomile essential oil: 2 drops

Camellia oil: 2 teaspoon

Instructions: Mix the oils and apply light upward strokes to the face, following cleansing, at night.

Nerve Tonic - Emotional Wear and Tear Blend

Lavender essential *Lavandula angustifolia* oil: 4 drops

Roman Chamomile essential oil: 1 drops

Coriander *Coriandrum sativum* essential oil: 1 drop

Instructions: Blend with one teaspoon of base oil and massage into your feet. Sweet almond oil, apricot kernel oil, sunflower oil, or grapeseed oil are suitable base oils with this formula.

Ingredients for Emotional Wear and Tear Blend. *Dorene Petersen*

Blue and Roman chamomile are powerful herbs and essential oils with a wide range of therapeutic uses. Blue chamomile is known for its stronger medicinal properties, especially for integrative oncology support, severe skin inflammation, sleep promotion, and gastrointestinal issues. With a pleasant aroma and taste, Roman chamomile flowers and leaves are favored for everyday relaxation and stomach upsets. Understanding their unique characteristics and benefits can help individuals choose the appropriate type of chamomile for their specific needs.

Whether used as tea, essential oil, or topical application, chamomiles remain trusted remedies for promoting health and well-being.

References

Al-Dabbagh, B., Elhaty, I. A., Elhaw, M., Murali, C., Al Mansoori, A., Awad, B., & Amin, A. (2019). "Antioxidant and anticancer activities of chamomile (*Matricaria recutita* L.)." *BMC Research Notes, 12*(3). Retrieved 6/10/24 from https://doi.org/10.1186/s13104-018-4041-2.

Cho, M. Y., Min, E. S., Hur, M. H., & Lee, M. S. (2013). "Effects of aromatherapy on the anxiety, vital signs, and sleep quality of percutaneous coronary intervention patients in intensive care units." *Evidence-based complementary and alternative medicine: eCAM, 2013*, 381381. Retrieved 6/05/24 from https://doi.org/10.1155/2013/381381.

Farhoudi, R. (2013). "Chemical Constituents and Antioxidant Properties of Matricaria recutita and Chamaemelum nobile Essential Oil Growing Wild in the South West of Iran." *Journal Of Essential Oil Bearing Plants*, 16(4):531-537. Retrieved 7/5/24 from https://doi.org/10.1080/097206 0X.2013.813219.

Gupta. (2010). "Chamomile: An herbal medicine of the past with a bright future (review)." *Molecular Medicine Reports, 3*(6). Retrieved 7/5/24 from https://doi.org/10.3892/mmr.2010.377.

Kimura, R., Schwartz, J., & Bennett-Guerrero, E. (2023). "A narrative review on the potential therapeutic benefits of chamomile in the acute care setting." *Journal of Herbal Medicine*, 41, 100714. Retrieved 6/20/24 from https://doi.org/10.1016/j.hermed.2023.100714.

Mann, C. & Staba, E.J. (1986). "The Chemistry, Pharmacology, and Commercial Formulations of Chamomile." *Herbs, spices, and medicinal plants: Recent advances in botany, horticulture, and pharmacology*. Vol 1. Craker L.E. & Simon, J.E. Editors. Arizona: Oryx Press, 235-80. Retrieved 7/12/24 from https://www.semanticscholar.org/paper/The-chemistry%2C-

pharmacology%2C-and-commercial-of-Mann-Staba/8682cbe36036e888bbe
39bbaecaf0ff54c786e28.

Mao, J. J., & Gubili, J. (n.d.). *Chamomile.* The ASCO Post. Retrieved
7/19/24 from https://ascopost.com/issues/may-10-2018/chamomile/.

Newall, et al. (1996). *Herbal medicines: A guide for health care
professionals.* Gurnee: Pharmaceutical Press, 69.

Sah, A., Naseef, P. P., Kuruniyan, M. S., Jain, G. K., Zakir, F., & Aggarwal,
G. (2022). "A Comprehensive Study of Therapeutic Applications of
Chamomile." *Pharmaceuticals (Basel, Switzerland)*, *15*(10), 1284.
Retrieved 6/2/24 from https://doi.org/10.3390/ph15101284.

Ullah, A., Munir, S., Badshah, S. L., Khan, N., Ghani, L., Poulson, B. G.,
Emwas, A. H., & Jaremko, M. (2020). "Important flavonoids and their
role as a therapeutic agent*." Molecules* (Basel, Switzerland), 25(22), 5243.
Retrieved 7/20/24 from   https://doi.org/10.3390/molecules25225243.

Zu, Y., Yu, H., Liang, L., Fu, Y., Efferth, T., Liu, X., et al. (2010).
"Activities of ten essential oils towards Propionibacterium acnes and PC-3,
A-549 and MCF-7 cancer cells." *Molecules,* 15(5):3200-10. Retrieved
8/2/24 https://www.researchgate.net/publication/45288373_Activities_of_
Ten_Essential_Oils_towards_Propionibacterium_acnes_and_PC-3_A-549_
and_MCF-7_Cancer_Cells.

Dorene Petersen is a New Zealand-trained naturopath and expert in
herbal medicine, aromatherapy, and holistic wellness with over 40 years of
experience. Growing up in New Zealand, Dorene developed a deep love for
plants and supporting wellness with aromatherapy and herbal remedies. In
1978, she founded the American College of Healthcare Sciences (ACHS),
an accredited institution dedicated to advancing integrative health education.

An advocate for accessible wellness, Dorene promotes the integration of
wellness as a daily habit. This philosophy has led to ACHS's partnership
programs, helping organizations adopt impactful wellness programs, and
promoting healthier, more sustainable workplaces and communities. She
has lectured worldwide on aromatherapy, medical herbalism, and integrative
health, with her work featured in journals like *The Herbarist* and the
International Herb Association's *Herb of the Year* books. Dorene has also
authored over 25 ACHS textbooks. Explore Dorene's writing and ACHS
programs and corporate partnerships at achs.edu.

Azulene is an aromatic hydrocarbon compound which gives the dark blue color to chamomile's essential oil. *Susan Belsinger*

Dried chamomile can be ground in a mortar and pestle, spice grinder or blender to prepare formulations. *Susan Belsinger*

A Balm for Aging Skin

Marge Powell

No matter what your age, your skin is aging. Though few of us pay much attention to this until one day, we notice physical evidence of this phenomenon. It is common that we first notice it in our face, and it is also common that our first reaction is panic. When I had this experience, I turned to my herbal library and found that while acne and other skin conditions were discussed, facial skin maturation was not. Turning to the internet, I found that the discussion of aging skin centered around skin cancers and chemical ingredients that I eschew.

As an herbalist, I set out to create a product I could use as a daily moisturizer that included ingredients traditionally used to benefit mature skin. I call the finished product "Chamomile Rose Facial Balm." I have now traveled 80 years and am pleased that this facial balm has been a daily companion for the past 25 years.

The Ingredients

Chamomile is an anti-inflammatory. In the presence of an anti-inflammatory, the skin is soothed, less irritated and less red. Chamomile has an abundance of flavonoids and phytochemicals which are known to fight against harmful free radicals and speed up cell regeneration, thereby improving the appearance of fine lines, wrinkles, and scars. An active ingredient in chamomile is bisabolol, which is not only anti-inflammatory, but anti-aging and anti-microbial. Bisabolol is extracted from chamomile essential oil and used commercially in many cosmetic products. It can be synthetically produced, but the synthesized product has been shown to be only 50% as effective as naturally occurring bisabolol.

Rose diminishes redness caused by enlarged capillaries because it has an astringent effect on the capillaries. While rose is astringent, it does not strip moisture from the skin. Roses contain antioxidants which help to strengthen skin cells, and in turn, can help regenerate skin tissues. These antioxidants also work to neutralize free radicals, which can provide anti-aging benefits to the skin.

Rosehip Seed Oil is unique among vegetable oils because it contains retinol (Vitamin A). Rose hip seed oil is high in the essential fatty acids linoleic acid or omega-3, and linolenic acid or omega-6. It is helpful for a variety of skin conditions, including dermatitis, acne and eczema, for mature and sun-burned skin as well as brittle nails. Rosehip seed oil is easily absorbed and hydrates and heals damaged skin. It also diminishes photoaging. It is used in combination with other oils.

Raspberry Seed Oil is anti-inflammatory and is high in essential fatty acids, specifically omega 3 and omega 6 which reduce the oxidative stress on skin.

Emu Oil also contains fatty acids that diminish acute inflammation and restores elasticity to the skin. Emu oil is a super moisturizer that increases skin thickness and can diminish age spots and wrinkles.

Wheat Germ Oil is high in vitamin E which is a natural antioxidant. It promotes the formation of new cells.

Almond Oil is an emollient as it softens, soothes, and conditions skin. It is also rich in protein and can help relieve itching from conditions such as eczema.

Avocado Oil is therapeutic and healing. It contains protein, amino acids and large amounts of vitamins A, D, and E.

Jojoba is a natural wax which forms a very thin, non-greasy layer on the skin which provides moisture control. Too much jojoba can clog pores on oily skin.

Patchouli Essential Oil is used in skin care, it regulates cellular tissue. Indicated especially for older skin.

Rose Absolute is cleansing, regulating and cooling. Recommended for mature, dry, or sensitive skin. It is also an antidepressant.

Vitamin E Oil is used as a preservative.

Garden roses drying. *Marge Powell*

Notes on the Ingredients

The chamomile must be dried flowers. It is difficult to grow and harvest enough chamomile in the average garden. Organic dried chamomile is available on the internet from reputable suppliers. When purchasing dried herbs, I always choose organic.

If you grow roses, the petals are easy enough to gather and dry and you can do it in batches until you get enough dried petals. A huge caveat is to only use organically grown roses that have not been sprayed.

The oils are available online or from your local health food store. Again, I would opt for organic if available. Emu oil is very expensive, but you will only need 2 ounces of it. It can be left out of the formula, although doing so sacrifices some of the benefits of the formula.

Rose absolute is also very expensive, but you need a very small amount of it as it will be infused in the jojoba in a 1:10 ratio. The smallest amount that is measurable will work.

The formula calls for beeswax, which should not be bleached. Natural beeswax is a soft caramel color. If you know any beekeepers, you can buy it from them, but it must be rendered first before you can use it. This means that it is heated in a crockpot; impurities fall to the bottom of the pot, and pure beeswax is poured off the top. It is also available online but be sure to get cosmetic grade.

Equipment needed

4 12-ounce glass jars with lids (for the infused oils)
Scale
4-ounce jar with lid (for the rose in jojoba)
heat source
1-quart saucepan
Instant-read thermometer
10 2-ounce glass jars with lids or 5 4-ounce glass jars with lids (for the finished product)
Hot pad
Funnel
Rubbing alcohol (to sanitize the glass jars)
Strainer

The Process: Part A

The roses and chamomile are used to infuse oils. This is a process that will take 6 weeks.

Measure 9 ounces of avocado oil into a jar; add 2 ounces of dried rose petals. Cover the jar. Shake the jar gently to make sure all the plant matter is in contact with the oil. Label the jar with the content weight and the date. Let sit for 6 weeks.

Measure 10 ounces of almond oil into a jar, add 0.8 ounces of dried chamomile flowers. Cover the jar. Shake the jar gently to make sure all the plant matter is in contact with the oil. Label the jar with the content weight and the date. Let sit for 6 weeks.

To make the rose in jojoba oil: note the weight of the rose absolute you want to use. Multiply 10 times that weight and that is the amount of jojoba that is put into a jar. Add the rose absolute to the jojoba and mix. This can be used immediately, or it can also be stored indefinitely.

Dried chamomile. *Marge Powell*

Chamomile Rose Facial Balm - The Formula

6 ounces rose-infused avocado oil
6 ounces chamomile-infused almond oil
2 ounces emu oil
2 ounces raspberry seed oil
2 ounces rosehip seed oil
1 ounce wheat germ oil
1 ounce jojoba
0.6 ounces vitamin E oil
2.4 ounces beeswax
1 ounce rose in jojoba
0.2 ounces patchouli essential oil

The Process: Part B

Decant the infused oils by straining them into a jar. Use a spoon to press the plant material against the strainer to extract as much infused oil as possible. Discard the plant material.

Weigh 6 ounces of the rose-infused oil and add it to the saucepan.

Weigh 6 ounces of the chamomile-infused oil and add it to the saucepan.

Add the emu, raspberry seed, rosehip seed, and wheat germ oils to the saucepan.

Add the Vitamin E oil to the saucepan.

Add the beeswax to the saucepan. Heat the mixture on medium heat but watch carefully; beeswax will melt at 160°F. Do not allow temperature to exceed 160°F. Remove from heat to cool slightly.

Meanwhile wipe the inside of the glass jars and lids with the alcohol (a spray bottle works nicely, too).

When the oil mixture is between 150°F and 157°F add the patchouli essential oil and the rose in jojoba. Mix to distribute the scent. Pour the mixture into the sanitized glass jars, using the hot pad and funnel.

Let the jars cool, cover with lids and label.

The jars can be stored at room temperature. I have stored them this way for up to 3 years. They can also be stored in the refrigerator until ready to use, which would extend the shelf life.

Chamomile flowers infusing in oil for Rose Facial Balm. *Marge Powell*

References

Gladstar, Rosemary. *Herbal Healing for Women*. Fireside, 1993. 235-236.

Knight, Dacy. *Byrdie's Beauty and Wellness Board*. "5 Skin Care Benefits of Chamomile." reviewed by Blair Murphy-Rose, MD, FAAD, https://www.byrdie.com/skincare-benefits-of-chamomile. Accessed 18 July 2024.

MacLeman, Elle. *The Derm Review*. https://thedermreview.com/bisabolol. Accessed 18 July 2024.

Powell, Marge. "Making Rose Soap." *Rose (Rosa) Herb of the Year 2012*. IHA, 2012. pp.191.

Rose, Jeanne. *375 Essential Oils and Hydrosols*. Frog Ltd., 1999. 124, 130-134.

Marge Powell has been an herbalist for over 45 years and an avid plant person her entire life. Her herbal interests span both the culinary, medicinal and body care as well as growing herbs. She completed a medicinal herb apprenticeship with Susun Weed and was introduced to herbal body care in workshops conducted by Rosemary Gladstar.

Marge is a passionate cook and most of her cooking is herb-enhanced. She teaches classes in cooking with herbs, bread making, making your own medicines, creating lotions and ointments, making soap, and blending scents. She has conducted hands-on workshops on these and a variety of other herbal topics across the United States. From 2000 until 2022, she owned and operated Magnolia Hill Soap Co., Inc., a producer of herbal soaps and ointments. In 2011 she created Magnolia Hill Nursery which wholesales organic herbs and heirloom vegetables to local garden centers.

She is currently a board member of the International Herb Association (IHA) and the International Herb Association Foundation and past president of IHA's former Southeastern Region. She has authored numerous herbal articles published in IHA's annual *Herb of the Year* publications. Recently she has begun collecting data on the history of folk medicine in northeast Florida and southeast Georgia, hoping to shed some light on this often neglected and unstudied aspect of herbal lore.

Chamomile ~ Herb of the Year 2025™

**Chamomile tea, then
Peter Rabbit went to bed
Dreaming of carrots**

Susan Belsinger

Bios for Illustrators and Photographers

Susan Belsinger—see bio on page 17

Gert Coleman—see bio on page 103

Kathleen Connole—see bio on page 25

Janice Cox — see bio on page 169

Pat Crocker — see bio on page 116

Rosemary Roman Davis — see bio on page 38

Karen England—see bio on page 144

Pat Kenny — see bio on page 116

Carol Little — see bio on page 205

Alicia Mann is a classically trained artist and metalsmith at Heritage Metalworks, LTD, in Downington, Pennsylvania. A graduate of Maryland Institute College of Art, she integrates her interests in art and horticulture by growing flowers, herbs, vegetables, and fruit trees. ammann1212@gmail.com

Dorene Petersen — see bio on page 226

Marge Powell— see bio on page 326

Jane Stevens — see bio on page 52

Gail Wood Miller is a member of the Musconetcong Watercolor Group and of the Garden State Watercolor Society. Drawing and painting have been hobbies since childhood. Her day job is health and education coach and consultant, focusing on women and children. A retired professor of English and English education, she also speaks and writes about individual learning styles.

Cover, Illustration, and Photo Credits

Front Cover:
Susan Belsinger

Back Cover:
Left/Right/Bottom: Susan Belsinger
Middle: Kathleen Connole

Section Covers:
The two most well-known chamomiles display different growth habits. Roman, *Chamaemelum nobile*, grows low to the ground; German, *Matricaria recutita*, grows much taller. *Pat Kenny*

Page Credits:
p. x: Chamomile has been used medicinally worldwide since before recorded history. *Gail Wood Miller*
pg 18-19: Bee, lacewing larvae, and butterfly on *Matricaria recutita. Gail Wood Miller*
pg 26, 44, 92, 190 & 237: German chamomile. *www.commons.wikimedia.org*
pg 53 & 82-83: Chamomile Dreams by *Alicia Mann*
pg 64: Peaceful chamomile blooms. *Susan Belsinger*
pg 66: Grateful Dead dancing bear. *www.clipartkey.com*
pg 74: Chamomile. *Gail Wood Miller*
pg 90: There are many accoutrements--from infusers & strainers--for making a simple tisane. *Susan Belsinger*
pg 104 & 180: German chamomile. Bartram's Garden, Philadelphia, Pennsylvania. *Pat Crocker*
pg 117: Glorious display of German chamomile flowers. *Pat Crocker*
pg 131 Sprightly chamomile in a bouquet of golden hues. *Karen England*
pg 132: Chamomile flower fairy dreams. *Kathleen Connole*
pg 138: *Gail Wood Miller*
pg 150: Tennessee warbler on chamomile. *www.commons.wikimedia.org*
pg 157: Chamomile, yarrow, and tansy are all bitter herbs easily grown in the home garden. Of the three, tansy belongs to the group of potentially toxic bitter herbs and must be used with caution. *www.plantillustrations.org*
pg 158: Chamomile flower girl. *Janice Cox*
pg 238: *The Tale of Peter Rabbit.* Beatrix Potter. *www.projectgutenberg.org*

Celebrating 30 Years
of Herb of the Year!

How the Herb of the Year is Selected

Every year since 1995, the International Herb Association has chosen an Herb of the Year™ to highlight. The Horticultural Committee evaluates possible choices based on their being outstanding in at least two of the three major categories: medicinal, culinary, or decorative. Many other herb organizations support the herb of the year selection and we work together to educate the public about these herbs during the year.

Herbs of the Year: Past, Present and Future

1995	Fennel	2013	Elderberry
1996	Monarda	2014	Artemisia
1997	Thyme	2015	Savory
1998	Mint	2016	Capsicum
1999	Lavender	2017	Cilantro & Coriander
2000	Rosemary	2018	Humulus
2001	Sage	2019	Agastache
2002	Echinacea	2020	Rubus
2003	Basil	2021	Parsley
2004	Garlic	2022	Viola
2005	Oregano & Marjoram	2023	Ginger
2006	Scented Geraniums	2024	Yarrow
2007	Lemon Balm	2025	Chamomile
2008	Calendula	2026	Turmeric
2009	Bay Laurel	2027	Flax
2010	Dill	2028	Basil & Tulsi
2011	Horseradish	2029	Nasturtium
2012	Rose	2030	Alliums

Books available on www.iherb.org

Join the IHA

Associate with other herb businesses and like-minded folks, network and have fun while you are doing it!

Membership Levels:

$50 Individual Professional
$50 Affiliate Professional
$50 Post Secondary Student

Log onto www.iherb.org to see what we are all about!

Membership includes:

Your business information listed on www.iherb.org
Membership directory
Herb of the Year™ publication
Quarterly newsletters
Online herbal support
Discounts on conference fees
Promotional support for IHA's Herb of the Year program and
    National Herb Week
Support for National Herb Day
Assocation with a network of diverse herbal businesses